SKINNY PIZZAS

by BARBARA GRUNES

SurreyBooks

Chicago

SKINNY PIZZAS is published by Surrey Books, Inc.,
230 E. Ohio St., Suite 120, Chicago, IL 60611.

First edition: 1 2 3 4 5

This book is manufactured in the United States of America.

Library of Congress Cataloging-in-Publication data:

Grunes, Barbara.
    Skinny pizzas : over 100 healthy, low-fat recipes for America's
       favorite fun food / by Barbara Maniff Grunes. — 1st ed.
       180 p.   cm.
    Includes index.
    ISBN 0-940625-57-1 (cloth) : $20.95. — ISBN 0-940625-54-7 (pbk.) : $12.95
    1. Pizza. I. Title.
    TX770.P58G78   1993
    641.8'24—dc20   92-38121
                                                 CIP

Editorial and production: *Bookcrafters, Inc., Chicago*
Nutritional analyses: *Linda R. Yoakum, M.S., R.D.*
Art direction: *Hughes & Co., Chicago*
Cover and interior illustrations by *Laurel DiGangi*

For quantity purchases and prices, contact Surrey Books at the address above.

This title is distributed to the trade by Publishers Group West.

Special thanks . . .
to Dorothy Grunes, Sharron Robbins, and Jane Tougus

CONTENTS

WHY "SKINNY" PIZZA?

P izza is perceived by many Americans as a special-occasion food. As with many such self-indulgent foods, pizza can be high in calories, fat, and cholesterol. But it doesn't have to be. This book will show you how to prepare great-tasting "skinny" pizzas—healthful pizzas with all the flavor and texture connoisseurs demand!

Fat contains more calories per gram than either carbohydrates or protein. Our "skinny" pizza recipes eliminate unnecessary fat—and calories.

Health experts have suggested that we be especially conscientious about limiting saturated fat consumption. Thus, the recipes in this book use only olive oil and canola oil, both monounsaturated fats. Actually, there is some scientific evidence linking monounsaturates to lowered blood cholesterol levels.

Remember that cholesterol is found only in foods of animal origin— not in plant foods such as fruits, vegetables, grains, and herbs and spices. Delicious "skinny" pizzas can be made with no meat and with low-fat or even fat-free cheeses.

1

Don't save pizza just for that special occasion. Easy, healthy, tasty "skinny" pizzas are a wholesome, delicious, anytime choice. And this health-sensitive cookbook will show you exactly how to make them.

Did You Know?

♦ *Pizza cheeses* are a source of protein, calcium, vitamins, and minerals.

♦ *Pizza crust* is made up of complex carbohydrates.

♦ *Pizza can be loaded* with an array of vegetables—all low in calories and high in vitamins and fiber.

♦ *All four food groups* are contained in one slice of pizza: grain, vegetable, dairy, and meat—providing a virtually complete meal.

INTRODUCTION

Pizza's explosion in popularity in the United States in recent decades must be one of the world's least kept secrets. It would be a rare American indeed who has not savored pizza in one of its myriad forms. In fact, the average American devours 7.5 pizzas each year; remember, this figure includes *every* man, woman, child, and baby in the nation. Pizza is rapidly closing the gap on hamburgers as America's number-one choice when eating out, and that does not include the millions of store-bought frozen pizzas, deli-prepared pizzas, and homemade pies.

Ironically, despite this incredible surge in popularity, pizza is still considered by many to be a "junk food." It is the purpose of this book to debunk that mythical belief and to provide recipes and tips that will allow the home-kitchen cook to create a wide variety of pizzas that have nutritional value, superior dietary character, and, especially, great taste.

"Skinny pizza" means lower-calorie, lower-fat, and lower-sodium pizza. However, two of the real joys of homemade pizza are the simplicity of preparation and the zesty, exquisite combinations of tastes. I have created and tested the recipes in this book with the consistent goal of combining both of those concepts—healthier pizzas that retain traditional tastiness and offer ease of preparation.

It has been my intention to design pizza recipes that everyone can enjoy, from the most finicky child to the omnivorous teenager, from the increasingly health- and nutrition-conscious adult to those with dietary limitations.

Skinny Pizzas does include a number of classic pizza recipes. I have, however, focused upon the use of "skinny" ingredients and preparation methods: thinner crusts, using lower-fat and lighter bases such as pita bread, whole-wheat flours, and even large crackers; low-sodium sauces and fat-reduced cheeses; and, finally, many unique "healthy" topping options such as nuts, fruits, and unusual yet readily available vegetables and ethnic foods.

I have also included dessert and party pizzas and a "Grilled Pizza Party."

Having lived for many years in Chicago, the city of pizza, I have experienced the pleasure of consuming my share of incredibly rich Chicago-style pizzas. I must say, however, that during the development of this book, I have become enchanted with the concept of "skinny pizza." Skinny pizzas retain the rich deliciousness of traditional pizza while being much more in tune with the emerging American diet. I am convinced that you, too, will be equally impressed by the taste, the flexibility, and the increased nutritional and dietary qualities of the recipes included in this book.

Viva la Skinny Pizza!

Before we get into the recipes, let's take a brief look at the history of pizza and at some facts about pizza as a full-meal food source.

A Brief History of Pizza

The exact origin of pizza is open to dispute. Some culinary historians even claim that pizza had its origin during the Neolithic Age, probably as a mixture of foods served with or on wheat flour crackers or bread. Pizza, as we Americans know it, evolved in Italy, probably around A.D. 1000 when the word *picea* or *piza* first appeared in the dialect of Naples. This early pizza referred to a round-shaped dough that was covered with flavorful ingredients such as olive oil, cheese, and bits of chopped vegetables and fish. Tomatoes, which are native to America, did not become part of the pizza formula until the sixteenth century, many years after the arrival of Columbus in the "New World."

Pizza, prepared and sold in open stands was popular in Naples for decades, and it became a favorite of kings and queens. It was offered to guests by the Bourbons at their receptions at the Palace of Caserta northeast of Naples. King Ferdinand IV had pizza cooked in the ovens of the famous porcelain factory of Capodimonte, and Queen Maria Carolina, sister of Marie Antoinette, had ovens built in the forests so she could enjoy pizza while hunting.

In 1889 the most truly recognizable ancestor of modern American pizza was created by the great pizzeria owner Don Raffaele Esposito in honor of Queen Margherita, consort to King Umberto I of Italy. This wonderful delicacy, known even today as "pizza alla Margherita," combined the colors of the Italian flag: red tomatoes, white mozzarella cheese, and green basil.

Italian immigrants to the United States brought pizza with them during the late 19th century. Pizza grew in popularity, spreading from Italy at the end of World War II, and becoming ever more popular in America.

American pizza has gone through various stages, from the Old Chicago period to the Nouveau California period. Today, pizzas, including many of those presented in this book, are often prepared "sans tomato sauce and mozzarella cheese" and topped instead with ingredients such as sun-dried tomatoes, fresh herbs, shrimp, goat cheese, and wild mushrooms.

Pizza on the Grill

A new, unique, and fun food is pizza on the grill. Pizza originally was cooked in outdoor, wood-burning ovens, so why not continue the custom. I am certain that you will be thrilled by the outcome of grilled pizza, and if you fail to try pizza on the grill, you will miss a great culinary treat and an exciting way to entertain. Don't fail to take pizza out of the "winter kitchen" and into the spring, summer, and fall air.

Any size or type of grill will do for pizza grilling. You can even use a smoker grill for a truly unique taste. Shape your pizza crusts to fit or complement the particular grill you are using. Try rectangular, square, or oblong-shaped pizzas. Your taste buds won't know or care what shape it was packaged in for delivery to your mouth.

The Ease of the "Piz"

Three of the most satisfying and delightful aspects of *Skinny Pizzas* are 1) the simplicity and ease with which these pizzas can be prepared; 2) the incredible diversity of pizza types and combinations that can result from some very basic crusts and sauces; and 3) the "fun" factor of pizza-making.

I have included several basic pizza crusts and sauces that can be prepared in advance and frozen in plastic wrap for later use. You can easily wrap portions of crust dough and sauce in dual pouches for individual pizzas, ready to defrost, add desired toppings, and put into the oven. Or, you can make entire pizzas, included in this book, complete with all desired ingredients and freeze them for instant use later, straight from the freezer.

Also, I have included numerous recipes that call for such commercially available crusts as English muffins, pita bread, crackers, etc., which are perfect for spur-of-the-moment occasions, unexpected guests, the midnight hungries, or whenever the situation demands an instant, delicious response.

Pizza-making can even be a participation sport for family and friends. Provide bowls of various ingredients, and let everyone top his own portion of the communal pizza. Or prepare individual crusts and allow your guests to go from there—as each person's whims direct.

Pizza, as I have mentioned, makes an absolutely scrumptious full meal in itself, providing a rich variety of tastes, textures, and aromas. You, your family, and your guests will love these meals, and everyone will walk away from the feast full, happy, and—particularly—healthy. And, I guarantee you, if you don't tell them it's "skinny" pizza, they'll never guess it!

1.
HINTS FOR THE BEST SKINNY PIZZA

♦ **Yeast** The recipes in this book were tested using both regular and fast-rise yeast. Either will work admirably.

Always check the date on a yeast package, and buy the freshest yeast available.

To activate the yeast, you may wish to substitute honey for sugar.

♦ **Dough** You may mix dough for crusts by hand or with a mixer or food processor. I tested all of the recipes in this book, using a food processor to mix the dough.

When setting the dough to rise, cover the bowl with lightly fitting plastic wrap and place a clean tea towel loosely on top of the plastic wrap to help retain heat.

♦ **Weather** can be a factor in the preparation of dough for crusts. Hot, humid days may cause the dough to be stickier than usual. To remedy this problem, add flour by the teaspoon or tablespoon, as needed.

7

♦ **Crusts** Be creative in the preparation of pizza crusts. For the most part, we have eliminated oil in the crust, so the character of the basic crust can be enlivened by adding various seeds and herbs such as sesame seeds, celery seeds, cumin seeds, and poppy seeds. Add seeds and herbs to fit the type of pizza you are preparing.

To cut calories, eliminate brushing the pizza crust with oil.

♦ **Vegetables** To saute vegetables with the least amount of oil, begin cooking the vegetables in a non-stick pan lightly coated, usually with about 1 tablespoon of oil or margarine. Cook covered, and stir vegetables occasionally until tender.

♦ **Pans** You may use a round or a rectangular pizza pan with equal effectiveness. Most of the recipes in this book suggest the use of a pizza tile. Always preheat the pizza tile. It takes about 10 minutes.

♦ **Baking** Always bake pizza on the lowest rack of the oven.

♦ **Freezing** Pizza freezes well, either cooked or uncooked. Wrap pizza with plastic wrap and then with aluminum foil or freezer wrap.

2.
INGREDIENTS FOR SKINNY PIZZA

♦ **_Crust_** If you are purchasing pre-made or frozen crusts, consider shopping the frozen bread-dough section of your supermarket. You may find some very interesting and unique doughs that will make marvelous pizza crusts. Experiment with various breads, crackers, rice crackers, muffins, and potato skins.

♦ **_Oils_** I strongly recommend the use of canola oil whenever possible and have called for canola oil as an ingredient throughout much of this book. Canola oil is extremely low in saturated fat.

Non-stick spray is effective for coating pizza pans and grill racks.

If you are using olive oil, always obtain the highest quality olive oil available.

Always use non-stick pans because it allows the same cooking results with a smaller amount of oil.

9

◆ **Margarine**   Avoid butter to lessen fat and calories. Choose a low-fat, tub-style margarine.

◆ **Flour**   Use unbleached flour.

◆ **Cheese**   Generally, select low-fat, low-cholesterol cheese. Grate cheese rather than using slices. This provides the cheesy flavor and texture but allows for the use of less cheese.

If you must use a higher-fat cheese, use less but in combination with a low-fat cheese.

Use freshly grated Parmesan or Romano rather than a store-bought variety. Store the cheese well wrapped in plastic in the refrigerator, and use when needed.

Please be encouraged to experiment with exotic cheeses occasionally to create pizza variety. For instance, try goat cheese or blue cheese but in combination with low-fat cheese.

Shredded or grated cheese will always melt more smoothly than sliced cheese.

◆ **Yogurt**   Yogurt is included in some recipes in this book, often mixed with ricotta cheese to make a tangy and creamy white pizza. Use non-fat yogurt.

◆ **Tomatoes**   I have called for the use of fresh, canned, or sun-dried tomatoes in various recipes in this book. Use Italian tomatoes for sauces and round tomatoes for slices. Make and freeze sauces during late summer when fresh tomatoes are plentiful.

◆ **Vegetables**   Canned or frozen vegetables can never equal the quality or flavor of fresh vegetables. Select fresh vegetable toppings as they become available in supermarkets, farmers' markets, or your own garden. Many fresh vegetables are now available in the United States throughout the year.

◆ **Spices**   If you do not already have one, I suggest you start your own herb garden outdoors or in an indoor flower box. In this way, you can obtain fresh herbs and spices throughout the year.

Many spices and herbs, such as basil, chives, and oregano, while superior in sauces, can also be sprinkled directly on top of a pizza to add extra flavor and color.

Have fun with spices and herbs. Again, experiment, or allow your family and guests to choose and use their own spices and herbs, according to individual taste. Don't forget exotic and regional spices such as Southwestern dried peppers and the wide variety of oriental spices.

◆ **Meats**   Choose your meat toppings by choice, of course, but I have recommended the use of turkey sausage and chicken breasts ground into sausage in recipes included in this book. Be sure to shop labels in your supermarket. New products, many with greatly reduced fat content and lowered calories, constantly become available on the market.

3.
EQUIPMENT FOR SKINNY PIZZA

Pizza-making equipment is pretty basic, although there have been several innovations in recent years that have simplified preparation and have made pizza more adaptable to a variety of cooking techniques and locales.

♦ *Pizza pans,* in a variety of shapes and sizes, are still the most common American-kitchen pizza-making implements. Most pizza pans need a very light coating of canola oil or non-stick spray. My non-stick 9 x 12-inch pans do not have to be greased.

♦ *Pizza stones and tiles* have become increasingly popular as a cooking surface. They can be purchased at specialty cooking stores. You can make your own tile pan, using a cookie sheet lined with unglazed quarry tiles, which you can obtain at a tile store.

11

♦ *Non-stick cookie sheets* work well for baking pizzas. No oil or corn meal is necessary.

♦ *Pizza racks,* or screens, are a recent innovation. I recommend the porcelain pizza rack from Griffo Grill, Quincy, Illinois. The porcelain pizza rack is ideal for grilling pizza outside on the barbecue grill, and it works equally well in your regular oven. The multi-holed surface of this rack allows more air to get to the crust, making your pizza crust lighter and crispier.

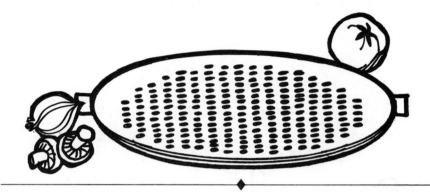

Other Recommended Equipment

♦ *A long-handled wooden paddle* is excellent for removing pizza from the oven and for serving.

♦ *Roller pizza cutters* are very useful; or use a home scissors reserved for this use.

♦ *Pot holders* or long-sleeved pot-holder mittens are essential.

♦ *A small rolling pin* works well for small or individual-size pizzas; use a heavy rolling pin for large pizzas.

Optional Accessories

A stroll through a cookware shop affords the pizza cook a tantalizing plethora of pizza equipment, much traditional and some innovative. I recently took such a stroll and here are some of the items I came across. Take a similar trip for your own pleasure.

♦ *Non-stick pizza pans* in a large variety of sizes and shapes, including:

> Deep-dish pizza pans
> Chicago-style pizza pans
> Thin-crust pizza pans
> Novelty-shaped pizza pans (Christmas trees, cowboys, Mickey Mouse, clowns, etc.)

♦ *Packaged pizza sets,* including pizza pan, cutting wheel, and pizza paddle (a good investment for the beginner).

♦ *Old World baking stones,* ⅝" thick, smoothly finished (you can use either side of the stone for baking).

♦ *Pizza paddle,* or peel, in solid pine.

♦ *Pizza rolling pins* in all sizes.

♦ *Pizza cooling racks.*

♦ *Home-kitchen pizza ovens.*

While a variety of pizza equipment is fun and convenient, really the most essential elements for creating superior pizzas are the ingredients themselves. If you have a fine-tasting crust, a zesty sauce, and fresh ingredients, your pizzas will be wonderful even if baked upon a plain cookie sheet.

4.
PIZZA CRUSTS

The basics of pizza are the crusts and sauces. This chapter presents the crusts, starting with the Basic Crust, that can be used with any skinny pizza recipe in this book. I have stressed the use of thin crusts for optimum healthfulness and reduced calories. In addition, I have included several optional crusts that can be tried for variety or that are suggested in some recipes. I want to emphasize that pizza lovers, like pie lovers, are very particular about the crust, and a perfect crust is an essential element of pizza making.

Remember, it might be necessary to add a tablespoon or two more of water, enough to make a dough ball. Do just the opposite if dough is too sticky; add a bit more flour.

BASIC PIZZA CRUST

Feel free to be creative with the shape of the crust. You can use a rectangle shape, square, triangle, or individual serving crusts. And remember, stoves vary, so bake the pizza until done, that is, the crust is firm to the touch and the edges are just turning golden.

24 Servings

Makes 2 (12-inch) round crusts;
or 2 (9-by-12-inch) rectangular crusts;
or 12 (6- to 7-inch) round crusts

½ teaspoon honey
1 cup (scant) warm water (110° F. or warm to the touch)
1 package active dry yeast
2¾ cups all-purpose flour (or bread flour, or a combination)
½ teaspoon salt
1 tablespoon good quality olive oil

To proof yeast, stir honey into water in measuring cup or small bowl. Sprinkle yeast over water and stir until yeast dissolves. Let mixture stand in draft-free area about 5 minutes or until yeast begins to bubble.

Meanwhile, mix flour with salt and oil in a food processor fitted with a steel blade, or in an electric mixer with a dough hook. (To mix dough by hand, use a bowl and a wooden spoon.)

Pour in yeast mixture and process until a soft, almost sticky dough is formed, about 5 to 10 seconds. If using an electric mixer, mix 3 minutes or until smooth dough is formed. If mixing dough by hand, mix ingredients until a smooth, slightly sticky dough is formed, about 3 to 5 minutes.

Knead dough by hand on a lightly floured surface or pastry cloth until smooth. If dough is too sticky, add flour by the tablespoon until it reaches the desired consistency. Put dough in a bowl and cover lightly with oiled plastic wrap and aluminum foil or a kitchen towel.

Let dough rise until it doubles in bulk, about 45 minutes to 1 hour. Punch dough down and let stand 5 minutes. Knead for a few minutes more on a lightly floured board or pastry cloth. Dough is now ready to use.

Nutritional Data

PER SERVING		EXCHANGES	
Calories:	58	Milk:	0.0
Fat (gm):	.7	Veg.:	0.0
Sat. fat (gm):	.1	Fruit:	0.0
Cholesterol (mg):	0	Bread:	1.0
Sodium (mg):	45	Meat:	0.0
% Calories from fat:	11	Fat:	0.0

WHOLE-WHEAT PIZZA CRUST

You can add various flavors to the crust to give it an extra special flavor. For example, you can add 2 tablespoons of honey mustard, lemon rind, curry powder, pesto sauce, and/or dried rosemary.

24 Servings

Makes 2 (12-inch) round crusts;
or 2 (9-by-12-inch) rectangular crusts;
or 12 (6- to 7-inch) round crusts

½ teaspoon honey
1 cup (scant) warm water (110°F. or warm to the touch)
1 package active dry yeast
¾ cup whole-wheat flour
2 cups all-purpose flour
½ teaspoon salt
1 tablespoon good quality olive oil

Proof yeast by stirring honey into warm water in measuring cup or small bowl. Sprinkle yeast over water and stir until yeast dissolves. Let mixture stand in draft-free area about 5 minutes or until yeast begins to bubble.

Meanwhile, mix flour with salt and oil in a food processor fitted with a steel blade, or in an electric mixer with a dough hook. (To mix dough by hand, use a bowl and a wooden spoon.)

Pour in yeast mixture and process until a soft, almost sticky dough is formed, about 5 to 10 seconds. If using an electric mixer, mix 3 minutes or until smooth dough is formed. If mixing dough by hand, mix ingredients until a smooth, slightly sticky dough is formed, about 3 to 5 minutes.

Knead dough by hand on a lightly floured surface or pastry cloth until smooth. If dough is too sticky, add flour by the tablespoon until it reaches the desired consistency. Put dough in a bowl and cover lightly with oiled plastic wrap and aluminum foil or a kitchen towel.

Let dough rise until it doubles in bulk, about 45 minutes to 1 hour. Punch dough down and let stand 5 minutes. Knead for a few minutes more on a lightly floured board or pastry cloth. Dough is now ready to use.

Nutritional Data

PER SERVING		EXCHANGES	
Calories:	57	Milk:	0.0
Fat (gm):	.7	Veg.:	0.0
Sat. fat (gm):	.1	Fruit:	0.0
Cholesterol (mg):	0	Bread:	1.0
Sodium (mg):	45	Meat:	0.0
% Calories from fat:	12	Fat:	0.0

YELLOW OR WHITE CORNMEAL PIZZA CRUST

The cornmeal crust was made famous in Chicago. The yellow and white cornmeal both taste the same, so choose your color. Cornmeal has a somewhat grainy texture and makes a thicker crust.

24 Servings

Makes 2 (12-inch) round crusts;
or 2 (9-by-12-inch) rectangular crusts;
or 12 (6- to 7-inch) round crusts

½ teaspoon honey
1 cup (scant) warm water (110° F. or warm to the touch)
1 package active dry yeast
2 cups all-purpose flour
¾ cup yellow or white cornmeal
½ teaspoon salt
2 tablespoons good quality olive oil

P roof yeast by stirring honey into warm water in measuring cup or small bowl. Sprinkle yeast over water and stir until yeast dissolves. Let mixture stand in draft-free area about 5 minutes or until yeast begins to bubble.

Meanwhile, mix flour and cornmeal with salt and oil in a food processor fitted with a steel blade, or in an electric mixer with a dough hook. (To mix dough by hand, use a bowl and a wooden spoon.)

Pour in yeast mixture and process until a soft, almost sticky dough is formed, about 5 to 10 seconds. If using an electric mixer, mix 3 minutes or until smooth dough is formed. If mixing dough by hand, mix ingredients until a smooth, slightly sticky dough is formed, about 3 to 5 minutes.

Knead dough by hand on a lightly floured surface or pastry cloth until smooth. If dough is too sticky, add flour by the tablespoon until it reaches the desired consistency. Put dough in a bowl and cover lightly with oiled plastic wrap and aluminum foil or a kitchen towel.

Let dough rise until it doubles in bulk, about 45 minutes to 1 hour. Punch dough down and let stand 5 minutes. Knead for a few minutes more on a lightly floured board or pastry cloth. Dough is now ready to use.

Nutritional Data

PER SERVING		EXCHANGES	
Calories:	58	Milk:	0.0
Fat (gm):	.8	Veg.:	0.0
Sat. fat (gm):	.1	Fruit:	0.0
Cholesterol (mg):	0	Bread:	1.0
Sodium (mg):	46	Meat:	0.0
% Calories from fat:	12	Fat	0.0

SEEDED PIZZA CRUST

◆

*Seeds such as sesame, dill, cumin, anise, and celery add
an interesting taste and texture to the pizza crust. Try using
your favorite.
If you freeze the raw dough or the baked crust, let it defrost
before baking.*

◆

24 Servings

Makes 2 (12-inch) round crusts;
or 2 (9-by-12-inch) rectangular crusts;
or 12 (6- to 7-inch) round crusts

- ½ teaspoon honey
- 1 cup (scant) warm water (110° F. or warm to the touch)
- 1 package active dry yeast
- 2¾ cups all-purpose flour
- ½ teaspoon salt
- 2 tablespoons good quality olive oil
  Canola oil, or non-stick cooking spray
- 2 tablespoons fennel seeds (or other seeds of
  your choice)

P roof yeast by stirring honey into warm water in measuring cup or small bowl. Sprinkle yeast over water and stir until yeast dissolves. Let mixture stand in draft-free area about 5 minutes or until yeast begins to bubble.

Meanwhile, mix flour with salt and oil in a food processor fitted with a steel blade, or in an electric mixer with a dough hook. (To mix dough by hand, use a bowl and a wooden spoon.)

Pour in yeast mixture and process until a soft, almost sticky dough is formed, about 5 to 10 seconds. If using an electric mixer, mix 3 minutes or until smooth dough is formed. If mixing dough by hand, mix ingredients until a smooth, slightly sticky dough is formed, about 3 to 5 minutes.

Knead dough by hand on a lightly floured surface or pastry cloth until smooth. If dough is too sticky, add flour by the tablespoon until it reaches the desired consistency. Put dough in a bowl and cover lightly with oiled plastic wrap and aluminum foil or a kitchen towel.

Let dough rise until it doubles in bulk, about 45 minutes to 1 hour. Punch dough down and let stand 5 minutes. Add seeds and knead for a few minutes more on a lightly floured board or pastry cloth.

Shape and stretch dough to desired pan size. Fit into pizza pan or pizza rack that has been oiled or sprayed with non-stick cooking spray.

Crust can be frozen raw at this point or baked and then frozen.

For baked crust, prick crust several times with a fork. Let rise 10 minutes in draft-free area. Bake crust on lowest rack in oven for 10 minutes. Cool crust on rack. Wrap and freeze.

To serve, bring crust to room temperature. Top and bake pizza at 425° F. for 20 minutes or until toppings are hot and cheese has melted.

Nutritional Data

PER SERVING		EXCHANGES	
Calories:	60	Milk:	0.0
Fat (gm):	.8	Veg.:	0.0
Sat. fat (gm):	.1	Fruit:	0.0
Cholesterol (mg):	0	Bread:	1.0
Sodium (mg):	45	Meat:	0.0
% Calories from fat:	12	Fat:	0.0

5.
PIZZA SAUCES

**W**hile not all recipes included in this book use them, sauces are truly a fundamental element of pizza. I have presented very basic pizza sauces in this chapter, but sauces can run the gamut of the human imagination. Be flexible and feel free to improvise with sauces.

I also suggest that you make a quantity of sauce during late summer or early fall, when herbs and vegetables are fresh and plentiful. You can freeze the sauce in quart containers for later use or give them as gifts.

The American Heart Association and the American Dietetic Association recommend limiting calories from fat to 30 percent of total calories over a period of several days. If we were to make *individual* food choices based on the "30 percent rule," however, we would never eat butter or margarine and never cook with oil—because these items derive 100 percent of their calories from fat.

For a healthful eating plan to be successful, it must be realistic and the food must taste good. Fat is a major component in creating taste and texture. And fat is a nutrient. Children need fat to grow into healthy adults. And even as adults, we need some fat in our diets. Unfortunately, most of us eat too much fat, creating a potential health risk for a number of chronic diseases—most notably, heart disease.

As you prepare the sauces in this book, you will note that some of them have a fairly high fat profile. But remember: these sauces are *ingredients*. You are concerned with percent of calories from fat in the finished product—the total pizza or, more precisely, a serving of the total pizza. Also remember that the realistic way to approach low-fat eating is to regulate your fat intake over *several* days. If you go overboard with the fat at one meal, balance it out with low-fat eating at your next meal or two.

If you consistently deprive yourself of the taste and texture of fat, your efforts to eat healthfully actually may be jeopardized. Strict deprivation often leads to a splurge. Splurges cause guilt. Eventually, guilt leads to just giving up. It is much better to enjoy eating and to allow yourself some freedom within a sensible, flexible plan of low-fat eating, over time, creating a food style you can live with, not a diet to suffer through.

Pizza is fun food—and it's flexible. With a little practice, you'll soon be making pizza an important part of your low-fat food style.

CHUNKY TOMATO SAUCE

This sauce can be prepared ahead of time and frozen. It is a good sauce to have on hand. Here's a special taste tip: add a small amount of honey to a tomato-based sauce.

24 Servings (approx.)

Makes 3–3½ cups

¼ cup chicken or vegetable stock
3 cloves garlic, minced
1½ cups onions, minced
1 can (28 ounces) crushed tomatoes
1 can (6 ounces) tomato paste
1½ teaspoons each: basil, oregano
2 bay leaves
½ teaspoon fennel seeds
1 teaspoon honey
½ teaspoon salt
¼ teaspoon pepper

Heat stock in saucepan over medium heat. Add garlic and onions and saute a few minutes until onions are soft. Mix in tomatoes, tomato paste, basil, oregano, bay leaves, fennel seeds, honey, salt, and pepper.

Bring sauce to a boil. Reduce heat to simmer, and continue cooking uncovered 35 minutes or until sauce thickens. Stir occasionally.

Discard bay leaves. Cool. If you are not going to use sauce immediately, put it in a covered container and refrigerate until needed. Stir before using.

Nutritional Data

PER SERVING		EXCHANGES	
Calories:	33	Milk:	0.0
Fat (gm):	.3	Veg.:	1.5
Sat. fat (gm):	.0	Fruit:	0.0
Cholesterol (mg):	0	Bread:	0.0
Sodium (mg):	314	Meat:	0.0
% Calories from fat:	8	Fat:	0.0

YELLOW TOMATO SAUCE

Let the sauce cool before using. Yellow Tomato Sauce thickens as it cools. In the fall, yellow tomatoes are plentiful, but if they are not available in your area, substitute plum tomatoes.

12 Servings

Makes 2¼ cups

   Canola oil, or non-stick cooking spray
3 cloves garlic, minced
¾ cup onions, minced
2 lbs. yellow tomatoes, chopped
2 yellow peppers, seeded, sliced
¼ teaspoon salt or to taste
½ teaspoon each: ground cumin, coriander, curry powder

Lightly coat a saucepan with cooking spray. In it, saute garlic and onions. Cook until onions begin to color, stirring occasionally. Add tomatoes, peppers, and spices. Heat sauce and reduce to a simmer. Cover pan partially and continue cooking 12 to 15 minutes, stirring occasionally. Sauce should begin to thicken.

Taste to adjust seasonings. Cool sauce. Place in covered container and refrigerate until serving time.

Nutritional Data

PER SERVING		EXCHANGES	
Calories:	23	Milk:	0.0
Fat (gm):	.3	Veg.:	1.0
Sat. fat (gm):	.0	Fruit:	0.0
Cholesterol (mg):	0	Bread:	0.0
Sodium (mg):	52	Meat:	0.0
% Calories from fat:	10	Fat:	0.0

RED BELL PEPPER SAUCE

Substitute green or yellow for the red bell peppers if necessary. Use this sauce as a base for pizza, topping it with sliced shiitake mushrooms, peppers, or some other favorite topping.

12 Servings

Makes about 3¼ cups

Canola oil, or non-stick cooking spray
5 large red bell peppers, seeded, chopped
½ cup red onions, minced
½ teaspoon each: garlic powder, ground cumin
¼ teaspoon each: salt, red pepper flakes, chili powder
1½ cups low-fat ricotta cheese

S pray a saucepan with canola oil. In it, saute peppers and onion until soft. Cover; stir occasionally. Stir in garlic powder, cumin, salt, red pepper flakes, and chili powder. Cool.

Pour mixture into a blender or food processor. Add cheese and puree. Place sauce in a covered container and refrigerate until ready to use.

Nutritional Data

PER SERVING		EXCHANGES	
Calories:	54	Milk:	0.0
Fat (gm):	2.5	Veg.:	0.5
Sat. fat (gm):	1.5	Fruit:	0.0
Cholesterol (mg):	9	Bread:	0.0
Sodium (mg):	100	Meat:	0.5
% Calories from fat:	41	Fat:	0.0

BARBECUE SAUCE

Puree sauce if you prefer smoother pouring. If you are grilling, you can cook this sauce on the grill. Set pan at edge of the grill to cook. Watch that it does not overcook, and stir often.

12 Servings

Makes about 3 cups

- 2 tablespoons canola oil
- 2 tablespoons garlic, minced
- ½ cup onions, minced
- ½ cup catsup
- 2 cups tomatoes, peeled, chopped, and seeded
- ½ cup chili sauce
- 2 tablespoons dark brown sugar
- 2 teaspoons chili powder
- ½ teaspoon Worcestershire sauce
- ¼ teaspoon each: salt and pepper

Heat oil in saucepan. Saute garlic and onions in pan until tender, about 4 to 5 minutes, over medium heat, stirring occasionally.

Mix in remaining ingredients. Bring sauce to a boil; reduce heat to simmer. Continue cooking 15 minutes, stirring occasionally. Cool.

Pour sauce into a container, cover, and refrigerate until ready to serve. Stir before serving.

Nutritional Data

PER SERVING		EXCHANGES	
Calories:	61	Milk:	0.0
Fat (gm):	2.4	Veg.:	1.5
Sat. fat (gm):	.2	Fruit:	0.0
Cholesterol (mg):	0	Bread:	0.0
Sodium (mg):	304	Meat:	0.0
% Calories from fat:	34	Fat:	0.5

6.
RED PIZZAS

"**R**ed Pizza" is the traditional pizza, containing tomatoes in one form or another and usually cheese. You'll find the basic cheese and tomato sauce pizza, but with a lighter, lower-fat and lower-calorie emphasis. Also, this chapter presents an array of innovative pizzas, using a wide variety of vegetables, herbs, seafood, and poultry. I think you will find these recipes zesty and tantalizing.

CHEESE AND TOMATO PIZZA

What could be more inviting than a hot, homemade cheese and tomato pizza made right in your own kitchen?

12 Servings

1 Basic Pizza Crust (12-inch)
2 tablespoons oregano
  Canola oil, or non-stick cooking spray
1 can (28 ounces) crushed tomatoes
2 tablespoons tomato paste
¾ teaspoon oregano
½ teaspoon basil
¼ teaspoon pepper
6 ozs. non-fat mozzarella cheese, shredded
4 tablespoons Parmesan cheese, freshly grated

Prepare dough on lightly floured pastry cloth. When kneading dough, mix in 2 tablespoons oregano. Shape and stretch dough into an oiled 12-inch circular or rectangular pan. Place dough on a pizza rack.

Drain tomatoes and mix with tomato paste. Mix in ¾ teaspoon oregano, basil, and pepper. Spread tomatoes over crust.

Sprinkle pizza with mozzarella and Parmesan cheese.

Preheat oven to 425° F.

Place pizza on lowest rack in oven on preheated pizza stone and bake 20 minutes or until done. Pizza is done when rim is just beginning to color. Serve hot.

Nutritional Data

PER SERVING		EXCHANGES	
Calories:	106	Milk:	0.0
Fat (gm):	2.6	Veg.:	0.0
Sat. fat (gm):	.7	Fruit:	0.0
Cholesterol (mg):	1	Bread:	0.5
Sodium (mg):	249	Meat:	1.0
% Calories from fat:	22	Fat:	0.0

MARINATED TUNA PIZZA

This is a good basic marinade. You can use it on most fish and shellfish. French string beans are sold in large supermarkets. They are thinner and tastier than their American counterpart, which can be substituted, if necessary.

24 Servings

Marinated Tuna

⅓ cup canola oil
5 tablespoons lemon or lime juice, freshly squeezed
2 tablespoons dill, chopped
3 cloves garlic, minced
¼ teaspoon white pepper
¾ lb. tuna, sliced into ½-inch strips

Pizza

2 Whole-Wheat Pizza Crusts for 12-inch pizzas
2 cups potatoes, just barely cooked, peeled, diced
1 tablespoon margarine
½ teaspoon garlic powder
1 large tomato, sliced
1 cup string beans, trimmed, blanched, and cut up
1 teaspoon each: tarragon, basil, rosemary
¼ teaspoon each: salt, pepper

Marinated Tuna: Mix ingredients, except fish, in a shallow glass bowl. Pour marinade into 1-gallon ziplock plastic bag. Add fish strips. Lock bag securely. Turn it several times so that all of the fish strips are coated with marinade.

Refrigerate and marinate fish 1½ hours. Drain.

Pizza: Meanwhile, prepare dough according to basic Whole-Wheat Crust recipe. Shape and stretch dough into 2, 12-inch oiled pizza or rectangular pans.

While fish is marinating, prepare potatoes. Melt margarine in a nonstick frying pan. Cook potatoes over medium heat, stirring often, until browned. Season with garlic powder.

Spread tomatoes on crusts. Sprinkle with potatoes, string beans, spices, salt, and pepper.

Prepare grill. When coals are hot, grill tuna, turning once, on a sprayed grill screen. Preheat pizza tiles about 10 minutes. Arrange fish on pizza crusts. Set pizzas on tiles. Cover and cook 5 to 10 minutes or until crusts are cooked and toppings hot.

Remove pizzas, cut, and serve hot.

Nutritional Data

PER SERVING		EXCHANGES	
Calories:	111	Milk:	0.0
Fat (gm):	2.5	Veg.:	0.0
Sat. fat (gm):	.4	Fruit:	0.0
Cholesterol (mg):	6	Bread:	1.0
Sodium (mg):	80	Meat:	0.5
% Calories from fat:	21	Fat:	0.0

Mahi-Mahi Pizza with Tomato Coulis

Never overcook fish; it is best when just done. The fish in this recipe can be substituted with fish of your choice.

24 Servings

Cajun Spice Mix

    1 teaspoon each: cayenne, diced minced onion
    ½ teaspoon each: freshly ground black pepper, paprika, garlic powder, salt, thyme

Pizza

    2 Basic Pizza Crusts (12-inch)
       Canola oil, or non-stick cooking spray
    1 lb. mahi-mahi
    ¼ teaspoon salt
    ½ cup green olives, sliced

Tomato Coulis

    4 cups tomatoes, peeled, seeded, chopped
    ⅓ cup red wine vinegar
    ¼ cup parsley, minced
    ½ teaspoon honey

Spice Mix: Mix all spices in a small bowl. Set aside.

Pizza: Shape and stretch dough into 2 oiled 12-inch circles or rectangles. Put pizzas on paddles lightly dusted with cornmeal or on oiled pizza tile.

Brush fish with spice mixture and salt. Grill or broil fish until just tender. Crumble into small pieces over crusts. Sprinkle with olives.

Coulis: Mix together tomatoes, vinegar, parsley, and honey in a saucepan. Bring to a boil, and reduce heat to medium-low. Continue cooking, uncovered, until sauce is thick, about 20 minutes. Remove from heat; cool. Sprinkle coulis over pizza crusts.

Preheat oven to 425° F.

Bake pizzas on lowest rack in oven, on preheated tile, 15 to 20 minutes. Crust will be golden and topping hot. Slice pizza and serve hot.

Nutritional Data, Mahi-Mahi Pizza

PER SERVING		EXCHANGES	
Calories:	87	Milk:	0.0
Fat (gm):	1.2	Veg.:	0.0
Sat. fat (gm):	.2	Fruit:	0.0
Cholesterol (mg):	12	Bread:	1.0
Sodium (mg):	103	Meat:	0.5
% Calories from fat:	13	Fat:	0.0

Nutritional Data, Tomato Coulis

PER SERVING		EXCHANGES	
Calories:	9	Milk:	0.0
Fat (gm):	1.0	Veg.:	0.0
Sat. fat (gm):	.0	Fruit:	0.0
Cholesterol (mg):	0	Bread:	0.0
Sodium (mg):	4	Meat:	0.0
% Calories from fat:	11	Fat:	0.0

RED BELL PEPPER SAUCE, ENOKI MUSHROOM, AND SHRIMP PIZZA

Shrimp, as well as most seafood, should not be overcooked. To cook shrimp, simmer them, turning once or twice. Shrimp are cooked when they turn a pinkish-white color and are firm to the touch.

12 Servings

1 Seeded Pizza Crust (12-inch)
  Canola oil, or non-stick cooking spray
2 cups Red Bell Pepper Sauce (see recipe in Chapter 5)
2 tablespoons margarine
2 cups small shrimp (if medium size, cut in half)
¼ teaspoon each: tarragon, white pepper, oregano
2½ cups enoki mushrooms

Shape and stretch dough by hand or with a rolling pin on a lightly floured pastry board into a 9 x 12-inch pan coated with oil.

Preheat oven, with pizza tile on lowest rack, to 425° F.

Spread Sauce over crust, leaving a small rim around the pizza.

Heat margarine in non-stick frying pan. Saute shrimp over medium-low heat until cooked, turning once or twice. Season with tarragon, white pepper, and oregano.

Arrange shrimp over sauce. Sprinkle bare spots with mushrooms.

Place pizza on tile and bake 20 minutes. Pizza is done when crust is cooked and topping is hot. Serve immediately.

Nutritional Data

PER SERVING		EXCHANGES	
Calories:	126	Milk:	0.0
Fat (gm):	3.8	Veg.:	0.0
Sat. fat (gm):	1.2	Fruit:	0.0
Cholesterol (mg):	46	Bread:	1.0
Sodium (mg):	184	Meat:	1.0
% Calories from fat:	27	Fat:	0.0

SHRIMP, TOMATO, AND OLIVE PIZZA

Lemon marinade, used in this recipe, is a good basic seafood marinade.

12 Servings

Lemon Shrimp

⅓ cup good quality olive oil
3 tablespoons lemon juice, freshly squeezed
¼ teaspoon white pepper
12 extra-large shrimp, peeled, deveined

Pizza

1 Basic Pizza Crust for 6, 6- or 7-inch individual pizzas
1 tablespoon lemon rind, grated
2 tablespoons margarine
4 small tomatoes, sliced
⅓ cup black olives, sliced and drained, or Greek oil-cured olives
¼ cup parsley, minced
½ teaspoon rosemary

Lemon Shrimp: Prepare marinade by mixing together olive oil, lemon juice, and white pepper in a bowl. Add shrimp, and marinate 30 minutes at room temperature. Drain well.

Pizza: Prepare dough. While kneading dough, add lemon rind. Shape and stretch dough by hand or roll it on a lightly floured pastry cloth into 6- or 7-inch individual pizzas.

Preheat oven to 425° F.

Heat margarine in non-stick frying pan. Saute shrimp on both sides until just done.

Arrange tomatoes atop pizzas. Divide shrimp and place over tomatoes. Sprinkle pizzas with olives, parsley, and rosemary.

Using a pizza paddle sprinkled lightly with cornmeal, quickly move pizzas one at a time onto preheated pizza stone.

Bake about 15 minutes or until pizza crusts begin to color. Remove pizzas with paddle and cut each in half; serve hot. You might want to serve extra olives with the pizzas.

Nutritional Data

PER SERVING		EXCHANGES	
Calories:	157	Milk:	0.0
Fat (gm):	4.4	Veg.:	0.0
Sat. fat (gm):	.6	Fruit:	0.0
Cholesterol (mg):	11	Bread:	1.5
Sodium (mg):	134	Meat:	0.0
% Calories from fat:	25	Fat:	1.0

CLAM, SHALLOT, AND GARBANZO BEAN PIZZA

Pizza with just tomato sauce and clams is delicious. Add shallots and garbanzo beans to create a fancy interpretation of a simple but tasty pizza.

12 Servings (6 individual pizzas)

1 Whole-Wheat Pizza Crust
Canola oil, or non-stick cooking spray
6 large shallots, minced
3 cups tomatoes, sliced
1 can (6½ ounces) minced clams, drained
1 cup red onions, thin-sliced
1 cup garbanzo beans, drained
½ teaspoon salt
¼ teaspoon pepper

Shape and stretch dough by hand or with rolling pin on lightly floured pastry board. Divide dough into 6 individual pizzas, 6 or 7 inches each.

Preheat oven to 425° F., with pizza tile on lowest rack.

Saute shallots in sprayed frying pan until soft, stirring occasionally. Dot shallots over pizza crusts. Arrange tomatoes, clams, onions, and beans on pizza crusts. Sprinkle with salt and pepper.

Using a pizza paddle lightly sprinkled with cornmeal, set pizzas one at a time on pizza tile.

Bake about 10 to 15 minutes or until pizza crusts turn light golden brown. Remove pizzas from oven and cut each in half. Serve hot.

Nutritional Data

PER SERVING		EXCHANGES	
Calories:	150	Milk:	0.0
Fat (gm):	1.9	Veg.:	0.5
Sat. fat (gm):	.3	Fruit:	0.0
Cholesterol (mg):	1	Bread:	1.5
Sodium (mg):	244	Meat:	0.5
% Calories from fat:	11	Fat:	0.0

ROAST CHICKEN PIZZA

This is one of those special recipes that uses leftover ingredients to advantage. In this case, the leftover ingredient is roast chicken. You could adapt this recipe for leftover turkey, fish, or slivers of meat.

12 Servings

- 1 Basic Pizza Crust (12-inch)
  Canola oil, or non-stick cooking spray
- 3 large shallots, minced
- 1 cup leeks, sliced
- 3 large tomatoes, sliced
- 2 cups roast chicken or turkey, boned, skinned, and chopped
- ¾ teaspoon rosemary
- ¼ teaspoon each: marjoram, salt, pepper
- 1 tablespoon orange rind, grated

S hape and stretch dough by hand or with rolling pin on lightly floured pastry board and fit into sprayed 9 x 12-inch pan.

Preheat oven, with pizza tile on lowest rack, to 425° F.

Spray a frying pan and saute shallots and leeks until soft, stirring occasionally. Cool. Spread cooled vegetables over crust. Arrange tomatoes over crust. Distribute chicken on pizza, and season with rosemary, marjoram, salt, pepper, and orange rind.

Place pizza on tile and bake 20 minutes or until crust is light golden brown and topping is hot. Serve immediately.

Nutritional Data

PER SERVING		EXCHANGES	
Calories:	104	Milk:	0.0
Fat (gm):	1.5	Veg.:	0.5
Sat. fat (gm):	.3	Fruit:	0.0
Cholesterol (mg):	16	Bread:	1.0
Sodium (mg):	108	Meat:	0.5
% Calories from fat:	13	Fat:	0.0

CHICKEN, TOMATO, AND SHALLOT PIZZA

To glaze shallots, first mince then saute them until cooked. Sprinkle shallots with sugar and continue cooking until they begin to shimmer.

12 Servings

1 Whole-Wheat Pizza Crust (12-inch)
  Canola oil, or non-stick cooking spray
2 cups Chunky Tomato Sauce (see recipe in Chapter 5)
1½ cups chicken breast, cooked, slivered
12 large shallots, peeled, minced, glazed (see instructions above)
1 teaspoon sugar (for glazing shallots)
¼ teaspoon each: oregano, basil

Shape and stretch dough by hand or with a rolling pin on a lightly floured pastry board into 9 x 12-inch pan coated with oil.

Preheat oven, with pizza tile on lowest rack, to 425° F.

Spread sauce over pizza crust. Sprinkle chicken and glazed shallots over sauce. Sprinkle with oregano and basil.

Place pizza on tile and bake 20 minutes. Pizza is done when crust is cooked and topping is hot. Serve immediately.

Nutritional Data

PER SERVING		EXCHANGES	
Calories:	151	Milk:	0.0
Fat (gm):	4.8	Veg.:	0.0
Sat. fat (gm):	.7	Fruit:	0.0
Cholesterol (mg):	12	Bread:	1.0
Sodium (mg):	304	Meat:	0.5
% Calories from fat:	28	Fat:	0.5

CHICAGO "SKINNY" PIZZA

In Chicago, my home town, hot pepper flakes, grated Parmesan cheese, and celery seeds are served at the table to sprinkle on the pizza. This "Skinny" interpretation of the famous Chicago Pizza has a thin crust, but the flavor is traditional.

12 Servings

1 Yellow Cornmeal Pizza Crust (12-inch)
  Canola oil, or non-stick cooking spray
2 tablespoons cornmeal
1 cup Chunky Tomato Sauce (see recipe in Chapter 5)
1 green bell pepper, seeded, chopped
1 cup onions, minced
½ lb. turkey sausage, remove from casing, slice thin
½ teaspoon each: pepper, garlic powder
½ lb. low-cholesterol mozzarella cheese, shredded, or non-fat cheese
¼ cup Parmesan cheese, freshly grated

S hape and stretch dough into a sprayed or oiled 12-inch round or rectangular pan dusted with cornmeal; or use a pizza rack; or cook directly on a pizza tile.

Spread tomato sauce over pizza crust.

Spray a non-stick frying pan, and saute pepper, onion, and sausage until crisply cooked, about 4 minutes. Season with pepper and garlic powder. Sprinkle vegetables and turkey over tomato sauce. Top pizza with mozzarella and Parmesan cheese.

Preheat oven, with pizza tile (if used) on lowest rack, to 425° F.

Bake pizza 20 minutes or until rim is a light golden color and sausage is cooked. Serve hot.

Nutritional Data

PER SERVING		EXCHANGES	
Calories:	167	Milk:	0.0
Fat (gm):	4.3	Veg.:	1.0
Sat. fat (gm):	.9	Fruit:	0.0
Cholesterol (mg):	19	Bread:	1.0
Sodium (mg):	471	Meat:	1.5
% Calories from fat:	23	Fat:	0.0

SAUSAGE PIZZA

The sausage in this recipe is homemade, thus avoiding the excess fat in the store-bought variety. You can make the sausage ahead of time and store it overnight or freeze it in a small, covered container. Pork is now raised leaner than ever before.

12 Servings

Homemade Sausage
- ½ lb. ground lean pork; discard any visible fat
- ½ teaspoon each: garlic powder, sage, orange rind
- ¼ teaspoon each: ground pepper, cumin seeds

Pizza
- 1 Whole-Wheat Pizza Crust (12-inch)
- 2 tablespoons orange rind
- 1 tablespoon margarine
- 1½ cups Chunky Tomato Sauce (see recipe in Chapter 5)
- ¼ cup non-fat (Alpine Lace) grated cheese
- ½ cup green onions, chopped

Sausage: To make sausage, mix pork with garlic, sage, ½ teaspoon orange rind, pepper, and cumin. Refrigerate in a covered container until ready to prepare pizza.

Pizza: Knead dough together with 2 tablespoons orange rind. Shape and stretch dough onto oiled pizza pan. Set aside.

Preheat oven to 425° F.

Heat margarine in small, non-stick fry pan. Add sausage and cook until pork loses its color. Mix in sauce.

Sprinkle sausage mixture over pizza and top with cheese and onions.

Set pizza on lowest rack in oven on preheated pizza tile or stone. Bake 20 minutes. Crust will be cooked when rim is a golden brown.

Nutritional Data

PER SERVING		EXCHANGES	
Calories:	110	Milk:	0.0
Fat (gm):	3.2	Veg.:	0.5
Sat. fat (gm):	.7	Fruit:	0.0
Cholesterol (mg):	9	Bread:	1.0
Sodium (mg):	157	Meat:	0.5
% Calories from fat:	26	Fat:	0.0

LEEK PIZZA WITH PROVENCE SAUCE

Leeks are a mild member of the onion family. They tend to be sandy between the layers, so wash them well under cold water.

12 Servings

Pizza

1 Whole-Wheat Pizza Crust (12-inch)
Canola oil, or non-stick cooking spray

Provençe Sauce

Canola oil, non-stick cooking spray
1½ cups tomatoes, peeled, chopped, and squeezed
½ teaspoon each: rosemary, tarragon, salt, pepper
2 cups leeks (about 1 large leek), well washed, sliced
½ teaspoon ground thyme

Pizza: Shape and stretch dough into oiled 12-inch pizza pan or onto an oiled pizza screen. Set aside.

Preheat oven to 425° F.

Provençe Sauce: Spray or coat frying pan with oil. Saute tomatoes over medium heat 2 to 3 minutes. Season with rosemary, tarragon, salt, and pepper.

Steam or poach leeks until just tender. Drain, sprinkle with thyme. Spread cooked leeks over pizza, leaving ½ inch edge. Drizzle sauce over leeks.

Set pizza on lowest rack in oven or on a preheated pizza screen and bake 20 minutes. Crust will be cooked when rim is golden and topping is hot. Serve hot.

Nutritional Data, Provence Sauce

PER SERVING		EXCHANGES	
Calories:	6	Milk:	0.0
Fat (gm):	.1	Veg.:	0.0
Sat. fat (gm):	.0	Fruit:	0.0
Cholesterol (mg):	0	Bread:	0.0
Sodium (mg):	91	Meat:	0.0
% Calories from fat:	12	Fat:	0.0

Nutritional Data, Leek Pizza

PER SERVING		EXCHANGES	
Calories:	70	Milk:	0.0
Fat (gm):	.9	Veg.:	0.0
Sat. fat (gm):	.1	Fruit:	0.0
Cholesterol (mg):	0	Bread:	1.0
Sodium (mg):	139	Meat:	0.0
% Calories from fat:	11	Fat:	0.0

CHICKEN AND SUN-DRIED TOMATO PIZZA

You can use slices of skinless barbecued or roasted chicken. Use sun-dried tomatoes, reconstituted in boiling water for 10 minutes. Drain, chop, and saute according to the recipe.

12 Servings
1 Yellow Cornmeal Pizza Crust (12-inch)
  Canola oil, or non-stick cooking spray
2 tablespoons margarine
3 shallots, minced
½ cup reconstituted sun-dried tomatoes, chopped
2 cups white or brown mushrooms, sliced
½ teaspoon each: chervil, salt
¼ teaspoon white pepper
1½ cups cooked chicken, slivered
2 ozs. Gorgonzola cheese, crumbled

Shape and stretch dough into an oiled 12-inch pizza pan; or use sprayed pizza rack; or cook directly on pizza stone.

Heat margarine in non-stick frying pan. Saute, covered, shallots, tomatoes, and mushrooms over medium heat until vegetables are tender, about 5 minutes.

Season with chervil, salt, and pepper.

Sprinkle vegetables and chicken over crust. Top pizza with Gorgonzola cheese.

Preheat oven to 425° F.

Bake pizza on lowest rack in oven 20 minutes or until crust begins to color and topping is hot. Cut and serve hot.

Nutritional Data

PER SERVING		EXCHANGES	
Calories:	114	Milk:	0.0
Fat (gm):	3.7	Veg.:	0.0
Sat. fat (gm):	1.3	Fruit:	0.0
Cholesterol (mg):	15	Bread:	1.0
Sodium (mg):	235	Meat:	1.0
% Calories from fat:	29	Fat:	0.0

SUN-DRIED TOMATO, THYME, AND BASIL PIZZA

◆

To reconstitute the sun-dried tomatoes, soak them in hot water, changing the water every 5 minutes, for a total of 15 minutes. Drain and chop.

◆

12 Servings

1 Basic Pizza Crust (12-inch)
  Canola oil, or non-stick cooking spray
4 cloves garlic, minced
¾ cup skim ricotta cheese
¾ cup sun-dried tomatoes, chopped, reconstituted
1 teaspoon each: thyme, basil

S hape and stretch dough by hand or with rolling pin on lightly floured pastry board and fit into sprayed 9 x 12-inch pan.

Preheat oven, with pizza tile on lowest rack, to 425° F.

Arrange garlic, cheese, and tomatoes over pizza. Sprinkle thyme and basil over all.

Place pizza on tile and bake 20 minutes or until crust is light golden brown and topping is hot. Serve immediately.

◆

Nutritional Data

PER SERVING		EXCHANGES	
Calories:	86	Milk:	0.0
Fat (gm):	1.9	Veg.:	0.0
Sat. fat (gm):	.8	Fruit:	0.0
Cholesterol (mg):	5	Bread:	1.0
Sodium (mg):	67	Meat:	0.5
% Calories from fat:	20	Fat:	0.0

Sun-Dried Tomato and Artichoke Pizza

Ricotta cheese is both smooth and creamy. A small amount is used to give the overall taste and texture of a creamy cheese. The cheese marries well with artichokes and sun-dried tomatoes. If fresh basil is available, use whole leaves and place them on the pizza just before serving.

12 Servings

- 1 Basic Pizza Crust (12-inch)
   Canola oil, or non-stick cooking spray
- 3 large shallots, minced
- ½ cup skim ricotta cheese
- ½ cup reconstituted sun-dried tomatoes, chopped
- 1 tablespoon basil
- 1 can (24 ounces) artichoke hearts, cut in quarters, drained
- 2 yellow or green bell peppers, seeded, cut in rings

Shape and stretch dough by hand or with rolling pin on lightly floured pastry board and fit into sprayed 9 x 12-inch pan.

Preheat oven, with pizza tile on lowest rack, to 425° F.

Saute shallots in sprayed frying pan until soft, stirring occasionally. Spread or dot ricotta cheese over pizza dough. Sprinkle dough with shallots, chopped sun-dried tomatoes, basil, and artichoke hearts. Arrange pepper rings decoratively over pizza.

Place pizza on tile and bake 20 minutes or until crust is light golden brown and topping is hot. Serve immediately. You might want to pass grated Parmesan cheese at the table for your guests to sprinkle on their pizza.

Nutritional Data

PER SERVING		EXCHANGES	
Calories:	108	Milk:	0.0
Fat (gm):	1.7	Veg.:	1.5
Sat. fat (gm):	.6	Fruit:	0.0
Cholesterol (mg):	3	Bread:	1.0
Sodium (mg):	109	Meat:	0.0
% Calories from fat:	14	Fat:	0.0

SOUTHWEST CHILI PIZZA

For extra flavor, serve this pizza with chopped onions and non-fat yogurt. Meat can be fine, coarse, or chopped; make it according to taste. Discard all unusable fat. Chili Pizza is good served with taco salad.

24 Servings

Southwest Chili

- 1¼ lbs. lean beef, fine or coarse-ground
- 2 cloves garlic, minced
- 1 cup onions, chopped
- 1½ tablespoons chili powder
- 2 teaspoons ground cumin
- ½ teaspoon oregano
- ¼ teaspoon red pepper flakes
- 2 cups cooked red beans, mashed
- 1 can (16 ounces) tomatoes, chopped, drained

Pizza

- 2 Basic Pizza Crusts (12-inch)

Southwest Chili: Saute the meat, garlic, and onions over medium heat in a saucepan until meat loses its color. Stir meat occasionally. As you stir, mix in chili powder, cumin, oregano, and pepper flakes.

Mix in beans and tomatoes. Bring mixture to a boil. Reduce heat to simmer and continue cooking 30 minutes. Taste to adjust seasonings. Chili should be slightly thick. Cool and drain.

Pizza: Prepare dough. Shape and stretch dough into two 12-inch oiled rectangular pans.

Preheat oven to 425° F. with pizza tile on lowest rack.

Spread 2 cups drained chili on each pizza. Bake pizza 20 minutes until crust begins to color and pizza is hot. Serve immediately.

Nutritional Data

PER SERVING		EXCHANGES	
Calories:	129	Milk:	0.0
Fat (gm):	3.7	Veg.:	0.0
Sat. fat (gm):	1.2	Fruit:	0.0
Cholesterol (mg):	15	Bread:	1.0
Sodium (mg):	89	Meat:	1.0
% Calories from fat:	26	Fat:	0.0

TOMATO AND SHALLOT PIZZA

Try this easy, versatile pizza for an appetizer. Cut it into small, easy-to-handle pieces and serve hot.

12 Servings

1 Whole-Wheat Pizza Crust (12-inch)
2 tablespoons dried basil
   Canola oil, or non-stick cooking spray
2 tablespoons margarine
6 large shallots, minced
2 teaspoons fennel seeds
½ teaspoon salt
¼ teaspoon pepper
3 cups tomatoes, sliced

Prepare dough. Mix basil into dough as you knead it. Set crust onto an oiled 12-inch round or 9 x 12-inch rectangular pizza pan. Set aside.

Preheat oven with pizza stone to 425° F.

Heat margarine in non-stick frying pan. Saute shallots over medium heat, stirring occasionally. Season with fennel seeds, salt, and pepper. Cook about 3 minutes.

Arrange tomatoes decoratively on top of pizza. Sprinkle shallots over tomatoes.

Place pizza on lowest rack of oven on stone, and bake 20 minutes or until pizza crust is just beginning to color and topping is hot. Serve pizza hot.

Nutritional Data

PER SERVING		EXCHANGES	
Calories:	82	Milk:	0.0
Fat (gm):	1.9	Veg.:	0.5
Sat. fat (gm):	.3	Fruit:	0.0
Cholesterol (mg):	0	Bread:	1.0
Sodium (mg):	162	Meat:	0.0
% Calories from fat:	20	Fat:	0.0

MUSHROOM, CAPER, AND SLICED TOMATO PIZZA

The type of mushrooms in this pizza is flexible. It's up to you. The choice can vary among white mushrooms, oyster mushrooms, brown mushrooms, or shiitake mushrooms.

12 Servings

1 Yellow or White Cornmeal Pizza Crust (12-inch)
  Canola oil, or non-stick cooking spray
3 cloves garlic, minced
2 cups mushrooms, sliced
3 tomatoes, sliced thin
4 tablespoons capers, drained
1 teaspoon each: thyme, oregano
¼ teaspoon each: salt, pepper

Shape and stretch dough into a 12-inch circle or rectangle, and place it in an oiled pan or pizza screen.

Preheat oven, with pizza stone, to 425° F.

Oil frying pan and saute garlic and mushrooms until mushrooms are just cooked, stirring often.

Spread mushrooms over crust. Place sliced tomatoes over and around mushrooms. Sprinkle with capers, thyme, oregano, salt, and pepper.

Cook pizza 20 minutes or until done. Crust will be golden and topping hot. Slice and serve pizza hot.

Nutritional Data

PER SERVING		EXCHANGES	
Calories:	67	Milk:	0.0
Fat (gm):	.9	Veg.:	0.0
Sat. fat (gm):	.1	Fruit:	0.0
Cholesterol (mg):	0	Bread:	1.0
Sodium (mg):	94	Meat:	0.0
% Calories from fat:	12	Fat:	0.0

EGGPLANT AND CAPER PIZZA

When developing recipes for pizza, it is only natural to adapt ideas using Greek ingredients. This is a very easy pizza recipe. If using dried herbs, use half as much as when using fresh because they are more concentrated. For example, use ½ teaspoon dried oregano instead of 1 teaspoon of fresh oregano.

12 Servings
1 Yellow Cornmeal Pizza Crust (12-inch)
  Olive oil, or non-stick cooking spray
1 cup celery, chopped
1 cup onions, chopped
2 tablespoons red wine vinegar
1 teaspoon sugar
1 12-oz. eggplant, trim stem end and discard, slice thin
1 teaspoon oregano
1 cup tomato puree
¼ teaspoon each: salt, pepper
2 tablespoons capers
3 ozs. fat-free, low-cholesterol mozzarella cheese, grated

Shape and stretch dough by hand or with rolling pin on lightly floured pastry board and fit into sprayed 9 x 12-inch pan.

Preheat oven, with pizza tile on lowest rack, to 425° F.

Spray frying pan and saute celery and onions until soft, stirring occasionally. Mix in vinegar and sugar. Cool. Spread over crust.

Meanwhile, spread out eggplant slices and sprinkle both sides with salt; lay on paper towels to drain for 30 minutes. Rinse eggplant quickly under cold running water. Pat dry. Set quickly under cold running water again. Pat dry. Set slices of eggplant over pizza. Sprinkle with oregano, and spread tomato puree over vegetables. Sprinkle with salt and pepper. Top with capers and grated cheese.

Place pizza on tile and bake 20 minutes or until crust is light golden brown and topping is hot. Serve immediately.

Nutritional Data

PER SERVING		EXCHANGES	
Calories:	89	Milk:	0.0
Fat (gm):	.9	Veg.:	0.5
Sat. fat (gm):	.2	Fruit:	0.0
Cholesterol (mg):	0	Bread:	1.0
Sodium (mg):	253	Meat:	0.0
% Calories from fat:	9	Fat:	0.0

SPINACH AND PLUM TOMATO PIZZA

This is an interesting sauce, rich, zesty, and colorful.

---

12 Servings
1 Basic Pizza Crust (12-inch)
1 tablespoon oregano
  Canola oil, or non-stick cooking spray
3 cloves garlic, minced
2 tablespoons basil
2 cups plum tomatoes, crushed
½ lb. spinach, washed, dried
½ cup cilantro or parsley
2 tablespoons extra-virgin olive oil
¼ teaspoon pepper
2 cups leeks, washed, sliced

Prepare dough on lightly floured pastry cloth. When kneading dough, mix in the oregano. Shape and stretch dough into an oiled 12-inch circular or rectangular pan.

Preheat oven, with pizza tile on lowest rack, to 425° F.

Saute garlic in sprayed saucepan until soft, stirring occasionally. Garlic should just begin to brown. Stir in basil and tomatoes. Chop spinach and stir into sauce. Mix in parsley, olive oil, and pepper. Simmer sauce 5 minutes, stirring once or twice. Cool. Taste to adjust seasonings.

Saute leeks in sprayed frying pan until wilted and cooked, but do not let leeks brown. Cool.

Spread sauce over crust. Dot pizza with leeks.

Place pizza on tile and bake 20 minutes. Pizza is done when crust is light gold and topping is hot. Serve immediately.

Nutritional Data

PER SERVING		EXCHANGES	
Calories:	103	Milk:	0.0
Fat (gm):	3.2	Veg.:	1.0
Sat. fat (gm):	.4	Fruit:	0.0
Cholesterol (mg):	0	Bread:	1.0
Sodium (mg):	68	Meat:	0.0
% Calories from fat:	27	Fat:	0.5

ASPARAGUS AND TOMATO PIZZA

Horseradish is grown mostly in the Midwest, with the majority of the harvest in Illinois. It is left in the ground through the winter and dug up in early spring. It is a very strong and flavorful root. Use with caution.

12 Servings

1 White Cornmeal Pizza Crust (12-inch)
   Canola oil, or non-stick cooking spray
2 cups plain non-fat yogurt
¼ cup skim ricotta cheese
2 tablespoons white horseradish, drained
¼ teaspoon white pepper
5 tomatoes, sliced
2 cups cut asparagus, cooked, drained
¼ cup fresh basil (if available)

Shape and stretch dough by hand or with a rolling pin on a lightly floured pastry board into a 9 x 12-inch pan coated with oil.
   Preheat oven, with pizza tile on lowest rack, to 425° F.
   In a bowl, mix together yogurt, ricotta cheese, horseradish, and pepper. Spread over crust. Arrange tomatoes over pizza. Sprinkle asparagus over tomatoes. Add the basil on top, whole or minced.
   Place pizza on tile and bake 20 minutes. Pizza is done when crust is cooked and topping is hot. Serve immediately.

Nutritional Data

PER SERVING		EXCHANGES	
Calories:	106	Milk:	0.0
Fat (gm):	1.5	Veg.:	1.0
Sat. fat (gm):	.4	Fruit:	0.0
Cholesterol (mg):	2	Bread:	1.0
Sodium (mg):	115	Meat:	0.0
% Calories from fat:	13	Fat:	0.0

FENNEL AND TOMATO PIZZA

Fennel has a mild anise taste and a crunchy celery-like texture. The fennel head looks like a short bunch of celery, with lacy green leaves. This vegetable is used in Italian and French cooking. If fresh tomatoes are not available, use canned Italian plum tomatoes.

12 Servings

- 1 Basic Pizza Crust (12-inch)
  Olive oil, or non-stick cooking spray
- 3 cloves garlic, minced
- 12 Italian plum tomatoes
- 1 large head fennel, about 1 lb.
- 1 teaspoon basil
- ¼ teaspoon each: sage, salt, pepper
- ½ cup Italian parsley, chopped

S hape and stretch dough by hand or with rolling pin on lightly floured pastry board and fit into sprayed 9 x 12-inch pan.
Preheat oven, with pizza tile on lowest rack, to 425° F.
Spray saucepan with oil and saute garlic until soft, stirring occasionally.
Skin and seed tomatoes. Puree tomatoes and set aside.
Trim stalks from top of fennel and reserve. Cut fennel into thin slices. Stir tomatoes and fennel in with garlic. Cover and cook over medium heat until fennel is soft, or fork tender. Cool.
Arrange tomato-fennel mixture over pizza. Sprinkle with basil, sage, salt, pepper, and parsley.
Place pizza on tile and bake 20 minutes or until crust is light golden brown and topping is hot. Serve immediately.

Nutritional Data

PER SERVING		EXCHANGES	
Calories:	90	Milk:	0.0
Fat (gm):	1.2	Veg.:	1.0
Sat. fat (gm):	.2	Fruit:	0.0
Cholesterol (mg):	0	Bread:	1.0
Sodium (mg):	105	Meat:	0.0
% Calories from fat:	11	Fat:	0.0

HERB PIZZA

Today the weatherman forecast the first freeze of the season, so we brought in all the herbs from the garden—and Herb Pizza was born! But if you do not have an herb garden, remember that most grocery stores now sell fresh herbs.

12 Servings

1 Whole-Wheat Pizza Crust (12-inch)
  Olive oil, or non-stick cooking spray
1 cup sun-dried tomatoes, reconstituted, shredded
1 cup red onions, thinly sliced
½ cup sage leaves
½ cup basil leaves
½ teaspoon black pepper, fresh-ground
¼ teaspoon salt

Shape and stretch dough by hand or with rolling pin on lightly floured pastry board and fit into 9 x 12-inch sprayed pan.

Preheat oven, with pizza tile on lowest rack, to 425° F.

Spread tomatoes and onions over pizza crust. Decoratively arrange whole sage and basil leaves over all. Sprinkle with pepper and salt.

Place pizza on tile and bake 20 minutes or until pizza crust is light golden brown and topping is hot. Serve immediately.

Nutritional Data

PER SERVING		EXCHANGES	
Calories:	70	Milk:	0.0
Fat (gm):	.7	Veg.:	0.0
Sat. fat (gm):	.1	Fruit:	0.0
Cholesterol (mg):	0	Bread:	1.0
Sodium (mg):	93	Meat:	0.0
% Calories from fat:	10	Fat:	0.0

BARBECUE PIZZA WITH GREEN PEPPERS

Using the Barbecue Sauce as a base adds new variety. Bell peppers and garlic are two natural ingredients to meld with the sauce.

12 Servings

(6 individual pizzas)

1 Basic Pizza Crust
1 cup Barbecue Sauce (see recipe in Chapter 5)
2 tablespoons margarine
3 large green bell peppers, seeded, sliced
½ cup onions, chopped
¼ teaspoon each: cumin seeds, pepper, chili powder

 Divide dough into 6 pieces. Shape and stretch it into 6 circles or squares, 7 inches each.

Preheat oven, with pizza tile, to 425° F.

Spread Barbecue Sauce over crusts; set aside.

Heat margarine in non-stick frying pan. Saute peppers and onions until tender, stirring occasionally. If vegetables begin to stick, add 3 tablespoons of chicken stock or water. Season with cumin seeds, pepper, and chili powder.

Spoon vegetables onto individual pizzas.

Using a paddle lightly sprinkled with cornmeal, move pizzas onto pre-heated tile on lowest rack in oven.

Bake until pizza is cooked, about 15 minutes. Crusts will be cooked golden brown and toppings will be hot. Cut pizzas in half. Serve hot.

Nutritional Data

PER SERVING		EXCHANGES	
Calories:	153	Milk:	0.0
Fat (gm):	3.2	Veg.:	1.0
Sat. fat (gm):	.4	Fruit:	0.0
Cholesterol (mg):	0	Bread:	1.5
Sodium (mg):	213	Meat:	0.0
% Calories from fat:	19	Fat:	0.0

MAXWELL STREET PIZZA

This morning my husband and I were walking through Maxwell Street, the Sunday open market area of Chicago. The aroma of the famous Maxwell Street hot dogs was wonderful. Here, Skinny Pizzas incorporates the flavors of that famous hot dog sandwich. Serve this pizza with a side dish of hot sauerkraut if desired.

12 Servings

- 1 Basic Pizza Crust (12-inch)
- 3 tablespoons celery seeds
  Canola oil, or non-stick cooking spray
- 2 tablespoons margarine
- 3 cups onions, sliced
- ¼ teaspoon salt
- ¼ teaspoon pepper
- 2 cups canned whole tomatoes, chopped, drained
- 2 tablespoons catsup
- ¾ cup (50% less fat) turkey links
- 6 cherry peppers, cut in half, seeded
- 3 half-sour pickles, quartered

When kneading dough, sprinkle it with celery seeds and proceed according to dough recipe. Stretch and shape crust into 12-inch oiled round or rectangular pizza pan. Set aside.

Preheat oven to 425° F.

Heat margarine in non-stick frying pan. Saute onions over medium heat, stirring occasionally until onions are soft and beginning to brown, about 5 minutes. Season with salt and pepper. Spread onions evenly over crust, leaving ½-inch rim. Stir catsup into tomatoes; spoon over onions.

Cut turkey links into thin rounds and sprinkle over pizza. Arrange cut peppers on pizza so that each slice will have a pepper.

Preheat oven to 425° F.

Place pizza on lowest rack of oven and bake 20 minutes. Pizza is done when rim is a light golden color and sausage is cooked. Serve pizza hot with slices of pickle and hot sauerkraut.

Nutritional Data

PER SERVING		EXCHANGES	
Calories:	111	Milk:	0.0
Fat (gm):	2.7	Veg.:	1.0
Sat. fat (gm):	.5	Fruit:	0.0
Cholesterol (mg):	4	Bread:	1.0
Sodium (mg):	225	Meat:	0.0
% Calories from fat:	21	Fat:	0.5

7.

WHITE PIZZAS

"**W** hite Pizzas" are any that do not include tomatoes. White pizzas, while not presenting the traditional red tomato sauce look, are delicious in themselves and can make their own dramatic and colorful appearance. Ingredients include everything from fowl and seafood to a full gamut of vegetables. Also included are basil- and goat's-cheese-based pizzas, which I am confident you will come to treasure.

CHICKEN AND BLUE CHEESE PIZZA

This recipe falls within the guidelines for "skinny pizza" because we use only a small amount of cheese and margarine.

12 Servings

(6 individual pizzas)

1 Basic Pizza Crust
2 tablespoons margarine
2 cups mushrooms, sliced
2 cups chicken breast, chopped
½ teaspoon sage
¼ teaspoon each: salt, pepper
⅓ cup blue cheese, crumbled
2 tablespoons walnuts, chopped

 Stretch and shape crust into 6 individual 7-inch pizzas. Sprinkle paddle lightly with cornmeal; set aside.

Heat margarine in non-stick frying pan over medium heat. Saute mushrooms and chopped chicken until just cooked. Stir occasionally. Season with sage, salt, and pepper.

Spread mushroom-chicken mixture over pizzas. Top with blue cheese and walnuts.

Preheat oven with pizza tile to 425° F.

Slide pizzas onto paddle, and with a long-handled spatula, move them onto tile.

Cook 20 minutes or until pizzas are done. Crust will be brown and toppings hot. Cut pizzas in half. Serve hot.

Nutritional Data

PER SERVING		EXCHANGES	
Calories:	152	Milk:	0.0
Fat (gm):	3.1	Veg.:	0.0
Sat. fat (gm):	.9	Fruit:	0.0
Cholesterol (mg):	12	Bread:	1.5
Sodium (mg):	193	Meat:	0.5
% Calories from fat:	19	Fat:	0.5

CHICKEN TERIYAKI AND PEPPERS PIZZA

Five-spice powder is just what it says: a combination of five aromatic spices. It is available at oriental food stores and most larger supermarkets.
To stir fry, move the food quickly with a spatula or spoon as it cooks.
If desired, you can add a special flavor to your crust by mixing in 2 to 3 tablespoons of sesame seeds while kneading the dough.

24 Servings
2 Basic Pizza Crusts (12-inch)
1 tablespoon canola oil
4 cloves garlic, minced
½ teaspoon powdered ginger
½ cup green onions, minced
2 cups bell peppers, sliced
1 cup white or shiitake mushrooms, sliced
¼ teaspoon each: salt, pepper, five-spice powder
2 tablespoons low-sodium soy sauce
1 cup cooked chicken, chopped

S tretch and shape crusts and set aside.
Preheat oven, with pizza tile on lowest rack, to 425° F.

Heat oil in wok or non-stick frying pan. Stir-fry garlic, ginger, and green onions 3 minutes. Add bell peppers and mushrooms and continue cooking, covered, 2 minutes or until done. Stir in salt, pepper, spices, and soy sauce. Mix in chicken. Cook 1 minute longer.

Arrange topping over crusts. Set pizzas on preheated pizza tile and bake 20 minutes. Pizzas are done when crust edges are a golden brown and toppings are cooked. Serve hot.

Nutritional Data

PER SERVING		EXCHANGES	
Calories:	72	Milk:	0.0
Fat (gm):	1.4	Veg.:	0.0
Sat. fat (gm):	.2	Fruit:	0.0
Cholesterol (mg):	2	Bread:	1.0
Sodium (mg):	113	Meat:	0.0
% Calories from fat:	18	Fat:	0.0

TURKEY AND ONION PIZZA

Here is another way to use leftover turkey. Only this recipe is a reason to make the turkey in the first place! If you want to make this pizza and do not have a fresh bird on hand, buy sliced low-salt turkey at the supermarket.

12 Servings

- 1 Whole-Wheat Pizza Crust (12-inch)
  Canola oil, or non-stick cooking spray
- 2 tablespoons margarine
- 2 cups red onions, thinly sliced
- ¼ cup beef stock, or water
- ¼ teaspoon each: pepper, nutmeg, allspice
- 1½ cooked turkey, slivered
- ½ cup low-calorie cranberry sauce, mashed

S hape and stretch dough by hand or with rolling pin on lightly floured pastry board into 9 x 12-inch coated pan.

Preheat oven, with pizza tile on lowest rack, to 425° F.

Heat margarine in non-stick frying pan. Saute onions 2 minutes; stir in beef stock or water. Continue cooking, stirring occasionally, until onions are tender. Season with pepper, nutmeg, and allspice. Mix in turkey slivers.

Spread onion and turkey mixture over crust. Dot pizza with cranberry sauce.

Place pizza on tile and bake 20 minutes. Pizza is done when crust is light golden brown and topping is hot. Serve immediately.

Nutritional Data

PER SERVING		EXCHANGES	
Calories:	114	Milk:	0.0
Fat (gm):	2.9	Veg.:	0.0
Sat. fat (gm):	.5	Fruit:	0.0
Cholesterol (mg):	12	Bread:	1.0
Sodium (mg):	95	Meat:	1.0
% Calories from fat:	22	Fat:	0.0

SMOKED SALMON AND CHIVE PIZZA

One Sunday morning while enjoying smoked salmon and cheese, the thought occurred, why not on a pizza? So here it is. You can use smoked salmon or cured salmon. Vidalia onions are a sweet, mild onion from Vidalia, Georgia. If Vidalia onions are not available, substitute any sweet, mild onion.

12 Servings

1 White Cornmeal Pizza Crust (12-inch)
  Olive oil, or non-stick cooking spray
2 cups Vidalia onions, thinly sliced
¼ cup grated Alpine Lace low-cholesterol cheese
½ cup chives, chopped
¼ lb. smoked salmon, shredded

Shape and stretch dough by hand or with rolling pin on lightly floured pastry board and fit into 9 x 12-inch sprayed pan.

Preheat oven, with pizza tile on lowest rack, to 425° F.

Saute onions in sprayed frying pan until soft and just beginning to color; stir occasionally. Cool.

Spread onions over pizza. Sprinkle cheese, chives, and salmon over onions.

Place pizza on tile and bake 20 minutes or until pizza crust is light golden brown and topping is hot. Serve immediately.

Nutritional Data

PER SERVING		EXCHANGES	
Calories:	84	Milk:	0.0
Fat (gm):	1.4	Veg.:	1.0
Sat. fat (gm):	.3	Fruit:	0.0
Cholesterol (mg):	2	Bread:	0.0
Sodium (mg):	144	Meat:	1.0
% Calories from fat:	15	Fat:	0.0

Mussel and Pesto Pizza

Cook mussels 5 minutes in a small amount of wine and water.
Discard any unopened mussels.

12 Servings

1 Basic Pizza Crust (12-inch)
   Canola oil, or non-stick cooking spray
¾ cup pesto sauce
24 fresh mussels, scrubbed, cooked, shells
    removed

S hape and stretch dough and place it on sprayed pizza pan. Spread pesto over crust with the back of a large spoon. Arrange mussels over pizza.

Place pizza on lowest rack of oven and bake 15 to 20 minutes. Pizza is done when rim is a light golden brown color. Serve hot.

Nutritional Data

PER SERVING		EXCHANGES	
Calories:	156	Milk:	0.0
Fat (gm):	4.2	Veg.:	0.0
Sat. fat (gm):	.6	Fruit:	0.0
Cholesterol (mg):	8	Bread:	1.5
Sodium (mg):	163	Meat:	0.5
% Calories from fat:	25	Fat:	0.0

MUSSEL PIZZA WITH GREEN SALSA

◆

Steamed, shelled mussels are mild tasting. In this pizza they are cooked on a bed of fresh green salsa. Use only opened mussels, discarding any unopened ones.

◆

12 Servings

Green Salsa

- 1 tablespoon good quality olive oil
- 2 tablespoons lime juice, freshly squeezed
- 2 tablespoons red wine vinegar
- ½ cup green onions, minced
- 1¼ cups cilantro, chopped
- ½ cup parsley, minced
- ½ teaspoon garlic powder
- ¼ teaspoon each: salt, pepper, red pepper flakes

Mussels

- 2 cups water
- ½ cup white wine
- 2 tablespoons lime juice, freshly squeezed
- 2 lbs. mussels, cleaned

Pizza

- 1 Whole-Wheat Pizza Crust (12-inch)
- ½ teaspoon garlic powder
  Canola oil, or non-stick cooking spray

Green Salsa: To prepare salsa, combine olive oil, lime juice, and wine vinegar in a small bowl. In a larger bowl, mix together remaining ingredients. Toss with combined liquids.

Mussels: Bring water, wine, and lime juice to boil in a kettle or other large pot. Add mussels. Cover, reduce heat to medium, and cook about 3 minutes. Discard liquid and any unopened mussels. Remove mussels from shells.

Pizza: Preheat oven, with pizza tile, to 425° F.

Shape and stretch pizza, incorporating the garlic powder, to fit a 12-inch round or rectangular pizza pan. Coat pan with oil or non-stick cooking spray, and fit crust into pan.

Spread salsa over crust; arrange mussels on top of salsa.
Bake pizza on lowest rack 20 minutes or until crust is golden brown.
Serve hot.

Nutritional Data

PER SERVING		EXCHANGES	
Calories:	172	Milk:	0.0
Fat (gm):	4.3	Veg.:	0.0
Sat. fat (gm):	.5	Fruit:	0.0
Cholesterol (mg):	16	Bread:	1.5
Sodium (mg):	216	Meat:	1.0
% Calories from fat:	23	Fat:	0.5

Clam and Chive Pizza

Canned clams are sold in most supermarkets, making this a most easy recipe. You can store the cans of clams in your pantry for a last-minute pizza.

12 Servings
1 Whole-Wheat Pizza Crust (12-inch)
  Canola oil, or non-stick cooking spray
4 shallots, minced
3 cloves garlic, minced
1 can (6½ ounces) minced clams, drained
½ cup chives, chopped
¼ cup grated Alpine Lace low-cholesterol cheese

Shape and stretch dough by hand or with rolling pin on lightly floured pastry board and fit into 9 x 12-inch sprayed pan.

Preheat oven, with pizza tile on lowest rack, to 425° F.

Saute shallots and garlic in sprayed frying pan until soft and just beginning to color; stir occasionally.

Dot shallots and garlic over pizza crust. Distribute clams and chives over pizza. Sprinkle cheese over all.

Place pizza on tile and bake 20 minutes or until pizza crust is cooked and topping is hot. Serve immediately.

Nutritional Data

PER SERVING		EXCHANGES	
Calories:	85	Milk:	0.0
Fat (gm):	1.2	Veg.:	0.0
Sat. fat (gm):	.2	Fruit:	0.0
Cholesterol (mg):	9	Bread:	1.0
Sodium (mg):	84	Meat:	0.5
% Calories from fat:	13	Fat:	0.0

ARTICHOKE AND "CRAB" PIZZA

Surimi, or imitation crab, is available at the fish counter at most supermarkets. In the Japanese process called surimi, fresh fish are processed, flavored, and reformed into a crab-like shape. It is then cooked. Most of the fish used is pollack, a saltwater fish found off the coast of Alaska. There is also some real crab mixed in, and flavorings, preservatives, and stabilizers are added to the compound. Surimi is much less expensive than crab.

12 Servings

1 Whole-Wheat Pizza Crust (12-inch)
  Olive oil, or non-stick cooking spray
1 cup red onions, chopped
16 artichoke *bottoms,* chopped, drained
1½ cup surimi, flaked
1 tablespoon oregano
½ teaspoon basil
¼ teaspoon each: salt, pepper
1 tablespoon Parmesan cheese, freshly grated

S hape and stretch dough by hand or with rolling pin on lightly floured pastry board and fit into 9 x 12-inch sprayed pan.

Preheat oven, with pizza tile on lowest rack, to 425° F.

Spread onions, artichokes, and surimi over pizza. Season pizza with oregano, basil, salt, and pepper. Sprinkle Parmesan cheese over all.

Place pizza on tile and bake 20 minutes or until pizza crust is light golden brown and topping is hot. Serve immediately.

Nutritional Data

PER SERVING		EXCHANGES	
Calories:	119	Milk:	0.0
Fat (gm):	1.2	Veg.:	1.0
Sat. fat (gm):	.3	Fruit:	0.0
Cholesterol (mg):	3	Bread:	1.0
Sodium (mg):	295	Meat:	0.5
% Calories from fat:	9	Fat:	0.0

WHITE PIZZAS

73

CAVIAR PIZZA

Caviar is sold frozen or fresh. Whitefish caviar is delicate tasting, a natural golden color, and a product of the Midwest. It is usually less salty than other varieties of caviar. Store covered in refrigerator for up to one week.

12 Servings

(6 individual pizzas)

- 1 Basic Pizza Crust
- 1½ cups low-fat, small-curd cottage cheese
- ½ cup plain, non-fat yogurt
- ½ teaspoon mace
- 1 tablespoon margarine
- ⅓ cup pine nuts
- ¾ cup green onions, minced
- 3 ozs. whitefish caviar

Divide dough into 6 pieces. Shape and stretch into 6 circles or squares, 7 inches each.

Preheat oven, with pizza tile, to 425° F.

Puree cottage cheese with yogurt and mace in blender or food processor. Spread mixture over pizzas.

Heat margarine in non-stick frying pan over medium heat. Saute pine nuts until golden brown. The nuts burn easily, so watch them carefully and stir often. Drain. Sprinkle nuts, onions, and caviar over pizzas.

Using a paddle lightly sprinkled with cornmeal, move pizzas onto preheated tile on lowest rack in oven.

Bake until pizzas are cooked, about 15 minutes. The crust will be a golden brown and the toppings hot. Cut pizzas in half and serve hot.

Nutritional Data

PER SERVING		EXCHANGES	
Calories:	187	Milk:	0.0
Fat (gm):	5.5	Veg.:	0.0
Sat. fat (gm):	.7	Fruit:	0.0
Cholesterol (mg):	43	Bread:	1.5
Sodium (mg):	329	Meat:	1.0
% Calories from fat:	26	Fat:	0.5

PEPPERS, GARLIC, AND ANCHOVY PIZZA

Peeling bell peppers seems like such a chore. But the taste is always worth the effort.

12 Servings

4 large red or green bell peppers
4 anchovy fillets, drained, cut in thirds
1 tablespoon good quality olive oil
3 large cloves garlic, minced
¼ teaspoon pepper
2 teaspoons capers, drained
1 Basic Pizza Crust (12-inch)
  Canola oil, or non-stick cooking spray

Char peppers on grill over hot coals, under broiler, or over gas flame. Turn continuously until peppers are charred on all sides.

Place peppers in plastic bags, 2 peppers per bag. Let stand 10 minutes. Remove peppers from bags.

Take off charred skins under cold, running water. Cut peppers in slices and place on flat plate. Scatter anchovies over peppers.

Heat olive oil. Saute garlic in small frying pan until beginning to color. Drizzle garlic over peppers and anchovies and sprinkle with pepper and capers.

Shape and stretch dough into 12-inch coated pizza pan.

Preheat oven to 425° F.

Bake pizza on lowest rack in oven 20 minutes or until done. Pizza crust will be cooked when light golden brown and topping is hot. Cut in slices and serve hot.

Nutritional Data

PER SERVING		EXCHANGES	
Calories:	78	Milk:	0.0
Fat (gm):	2.0	Veg.:	0.0
Sat. fat (gm):	.3	Fruit:	0.0
Cholesterol (mg):	1	Bread:	1.0
Sodium (mg):	94	Meat:	0.0
% Calories from fat:	23	Fat:	0.0

STIR-FRY ORIENTAL PIZZA

Oriental sesame seed oil and sliced shiitake (dried) mushrooms are available at Asian markets or large supermarkets. To reconstitute dried mushrooms, soak them in hot water 15 minutes or until soft. Drain.

12 Servings

Pizza
- 1 White Cornmeal Pizza Crust (12-inch)
  Canola oil, or non-stick cooking spray

Sauce
- 2 tablespoons light soy sauce
- 2 tablespoons dry white wine
- 1 tablespoon cider vinegar
- 2 teaspoons oriental sesame seed oil
- ½ teaspoon each: salt, cornstarch mixed with 2 tablespoons water

Vegetables
- 2 tablespoons canola oil
- 3 cloves garlic, minced
- 5 green onions, sliced in half horizontally, cut into ½-inch pieces
- ½ cup shiitake mushrooms, reconstituted, sliced
- 2 yellow peppers, seeded, sliced
- ¾ cup snow peas, trimmed
- ½ teaspoon each: red chili flakes, salt, ground ginger

Pizza: Shape and stretch dough into 12-inch pizza pan coated with oil or non-stick cooking spray.

Sauce: Mix sauce ingredients together in small bowl. Set aside.

Vegetables: Heat oil, garlic, and onions in wok or non-stick frying pan. Add mushrooms, peppers, and snow peas and stir-fry until tender.

Stir in sauce and seasonings. Spread mixture over crust.

Preheat oven to 425° degrees F.

Bake pizza on lowest rack in oven 20 minutes or until crust is cooked and topping hot.

Cut into slices and serve hot.

Nutritional Data

PER SERVING		EXCHANGES	
Calories:	139	Milk:	0.0
Fat (gm):	3.0	Veg.:	0.0
Sat. fat (gm):	.3	Fruit:	0.0
Cholesterol (mg):	0	Bread:	1.5
Sodium (mg):	181	Meat:	0.0
% Calories from fat:	19	Fat:	0.5

BOK CHOY AND TOFU PIZZA

Use oriental sesame seed oil when preparing oriental dishes. It is available at large supermarkets and from oriental and Asian food or specialty stores.

12 Servings

1 Basic Pizza Crust (12-inch)
  Canola oil, or non-stick cooking spray
1 tablespoon canola oil
3 large cloves garlic, minced
1 teaspoon ginger, grated
3 cups bok choy, thinly sliced
½ teaspoon salt
¼ teaspoon red pepper flakes (or to taste)
½ teaspoon sesame oil (or to taste)
2 cups firm tofu, cut into ½-inch cubes

S hape and stretch dough into a 12-inch circle or rectangle, and place it on sprayed pan or pizza screen.

Preheat oven to 425° F., with pizza tile on lowest rack.

Heat 1 tablespoon oil in frying pan with garlic and ginger. Cook 1 minute over medium heat, stirring often. Mix in bok choy and stir fry. Use a spatula or spoon to move the food quickly as vegetables cook. Bok choy will wilt and cook quickly. Remove from heat. Season with salt, pepper flakes, and sesame oil.

Arrange bok choy over pizza and sprinkle with tofu.

Place pizza on lowest rack of oven on preheated pizza tile and bake 20 minutes. Pizza is done when the rim is a light golden brown color. Serve hot.

Nutritional Data

PER SERVING		EXCHANGES	
Calories:	194	Milk:	0.0
Fat (gm):	6.4	Veg.:	0.0
Sat. fat (gm):	.8	Fruit:	0.0
Cholesterol (mg):	0	Bread:	1.0
Sodium (mg):	189	Meat:	1.0
% Calories from fat:	29	Fat:	1.0

SPINACH AND CHEESE PIZZA

Spinach has a slightly bitter taste due to the stem. If it bothers you, simply cut out the stems.

12 Servings

1 package frozen bread dough, thawed
  Canola oil, or non-stick cooking spray
3 cloves garlic, minced
1 cup onions, sliced
1 lb. frozen spinach, cleaned, trimmed, chopped
2 teaspoons dill
¼ teaspoon pepper
½ lb. low-fat, small-curd cottage cheese, pureed

Divide dough into 6 equal pieces. On a lightly floured board, shape and stretch each ball of dough into a circle, about 6 inches in diameter.

Oil or spray a large non-stick frying pan.

Saute garlic and onions 4 minutes or until onions are soft. Stir in spinach. Cover and continue cooking over medium heat, stirring once or twice until spinach has wilted. Season with dill and pepper. Mix in cheese.

Arrange spinach mixture over pizzas, leaving a ½-inch rim.

When coals are hot and pizza tile is preheated, begin grilling. Place pizza on grill using paddle sprinkled lightly with cornmeal. Cover grill and cook about 5 minutes or until pizza is cooked. Crust will be hot and beginning to color.

(Alternative directions for cooking in oven: Preheat oven to 425° F. Move pizza onto preheated tile on lowest rack in oven. Bake until pizza is cooked, about 15 minutes or when crusts turn a golden color.)

Using a long-handled spatula, remove pizza onto paddle. Place on serving dish, cut in halves, and serve.

Nutritional Data

PER SERVING		EXCHANGES	
Calories:	124	Milk:	0.0
Fat (gm):	3.0	Veg.:	1.0
Sat. fat (gm):	.1	Fruit:	0.0
Cholesterol (mg):	1	Bread:	1.0
Sodium (mg):	337	Meat:	0.5
% Calories from fat:	20	Fat:	0.0

SPINACH, GARBANZO BEAN, AND PIMIENTO PIZZA

An interesting combination of tastes and textures. Garbanzo beans come canned; just drain and use.

12 Servings

1 Whole-Wheat Pizza Crust (12-inch)
  Canola oil, or non-stick cooking spray
1 tablespoon good quality olive oil
3 cloves garlic, minced
1 cup onions, thinly sliced
1 package (10 ounces) chopped spinach, defrosted, well drained
½ teaspoon tarragon
¼ teaspoon pepper
1 jar (2½ ounces) chopped pimiento, drained
½ cup garbanzo beans, drained
½ cup low-fat mozzarella cheese, shredded

S hape and stretch dough into an oiled 12-inch pizza pan, or use a sprayed grill rack.

Preheat oven, with pizza tile, to 425° F.

Heat olive oil in frying pan. Saute garlic and onion over medium heat until onion is tender, about 4 minutes. Add spinach, tarragon, and pepper. Cover and continue cooking about 5 to 7 minutes until spinach is dry.

Spoon and spread vegetables on pizza crust, leaving ½-inch rim. Sprinkle pimiento and garbanzo beans over pizza. Sprinkle cheese over top.

Place pizza on lowest rack of oven on preheated pizza tile and bake 20 minutes. Pizza is done when rim is light golden brown. Serve hot.

Nutritional Data

PER SERVING		EXCHANGES	
Calories:	165	Milk:	0.0
Fat (gm):	3.5	Veg.:	0.5
Sat. fat (gm):	.4	Fruit:	0.0
Cholesterol (mg):	3	Bread:	1.5
Sodium (mg):	169	Meat:	0.5
% Calories from fat:	19	Fat:	0.5

ZUCCHINI, SQUASH, AND FENNEL SEED PIZZA

Be sure to make this pizza in the fall when both zucchini and squash are plentiful.

12 Servings

1 Cornmeal Pizza Crust (12-inch)
  Canola oil, or non-stick cooking spray
4 cloves garlic, sliced into slivers
¾ cup green onions, chopped
1½ cups small, firm zucchini, sliced
1 cup yellow squash, sliced
¾ teaspoon fennel seeds
¼ teaspoon each: salt, pepper, oregano
⅓ cup fat-free, low-cholesterol mozzarella cheese, grated

S hape and stretch dough by hand or with rolling pin on lightly floured pastry board and fit into sprayed 9 x 12-inch pan.
Preheat oven, with pizza tile on lowest rack, to 425° F.

Spray pan and saute garlic and green onions until soft, stirring occasionally. Add zucchini and squash and saute lightly, about 2 minutes. Turn vegetables over, using spatula, and saute another 1 minute. Cool. Arrange vegetables decoratively over pizza. Season with fennel seeds, salt, pepper, and oregano. Sprinkle cheese over all.

Place pizza on tile and bake 20 minutes or until crust is light golden brown and topping is hot. Serve immediately.

Nutritional Data

PER SERVING		EXCHANGES	
Calories:	72	Milk:	0.0
Fat (gm):	.9	Veg.:	0.0
Sat. fat (gm):	.1	Fruit:	0.0
Cholesterol (mg):	0	Bread:	1.0
Sodium (mg):	122	Meat:	0.0
% Calories from fat:	12	Fat:	0.0

GARDEN PIZZA

This pizza is only limited by your imagination. Be creative and add your favorite vegetables—feel free to substitute for any of those listed below.

12 Servings

1 White Cornmeal Pizza Crust (12-inch)
  Olive oil, or non-stick cooking spray
1 cup zucchini, thinly sliced
1 cup onions, thinly sliced
1 cup leeks, thinly sliced
½ cup carrots, thinly sliced
½ teaspoon each: black pepper, grated
  lemon rind

Shape and stretch dough by hand or with rolling pin on lightly floured pastry board and fit into 9 x 12-inch sprayed pan.

Preheat oven, with pizza tile on lowest rack, to 425° F.

Arrange vegetables decoratively over pizza. Sprinkle with pepper and grated lemon rind.

Place pizza on tile and bake 20 minutes. Pizza is done when crust is light golden brown and topping is hot. Serve immediately.

Nutritional Data

PER SERVING		EXCHANGES	
Calories:	73	Milk:	0.0
Fat (gm):	.9	Veg.:	0.0
Sat. fat (gm):	.1	Fruit:	0.0
Cholesterol (mg):	0	Bread:	1.0
Sodium (mg):	50	Meat:	0.0
% Calories from fat:	11	Fat:	0.0

VEGETABLE PIZZA

The leek is a more gentle member of the onion family. A favorite French vegetable, it now stretches to crown an Italian pizza made in America. It is usually very sandy, so wash well before slicing.

12 Servings

1 Yellow Cornmeal Pizza Crust (12-inch)
  Canola oil, or non-stick cooking spray
2 tablespoons margarine
4 cups leeks, white portion only, washed, sliced
⅓ cup chicken stock
1 tablespoon dry white wine
1 cup cooked carrots, sliced, drained
1 teaspoon lemon rind, grated
¼ teaspoon each: white pepper, ground ginger, ground mace

Shape and stretch dough by hand or with rolling pin on lightly floured pastry board into 9 x 12-inch coated pan.

Preheat oven, with pizza tile on lowest rack, to 425° F.

Heat margarine in non-stick frying pan. Saute leeks for 1 to 2 minutes. Stir in chicken stock and wine. Continue cooking, stirring occasionally, until tender. Mix in carrots, lemon rind, white pepper, ginger, and mace.

Spread vegetable mixture over crust, leaving a small rim around the pizza.

Place pizza on tile and bake 20 minutes. Pizza is done when crust is light golden brown and topping is hot. Serve immediately.

Nutritional Data

PER SERVING		EXCHANGES	
Calories:	97	Milk:	0.0
Fat (gm):	1.9	Veg.:	1.0
Sat. fat (gm):	.3	Fruit:	0.0
Cholesterol (mg):	0	Bread:	1.0
Sodium (mg):	101	Meat:	0.0
% Calories from fat:	17	Fat:	0.0

EGGPLANT AND TWO-CHEESE PIZZA

Oriental eggplants are small in shape, white or purple in color, and available at oriental food markets and most larger supermarkets. Use regular eggplants if the oriental variety are not available.

24 Servings

4 Oriental eggplants, trimmed, cut horizontally into ½-inch pieces
Canola oil, or non-stick cooking spray
2 cloves garlic, divided
1 cup onions (about 2 onions), minced
2 Whole-Wheat pizza Crusts (12-inch)
Canola oil, or non-stick cooking spray
2 cups skim ricotta cheese
½ teaspoon each: marjoram, dill, salt
¼ teaspoon pepper
½ cup Parmesan or Romano cheese, freshly grated

S prinkle eggplants with salt, and let stand 20 minutes on paper towels. Rinse off salt and pat dry with more paper towels.

Oil or spray a non-stick frying pan. Over medium heat, saute eggplant slices 2 minutes on each side until they begin to color. Remove from pan.

Saute onion and garlic 4 to 5 minutes, stirring occasionally. Set aside. If onions are dry, add 3 tablespoons chicken stock.

Shape and stretch dough into 2, 12-inch pans coated with oil or sprayed with non-stick cooking spray.

Spread ricotta cheese on crust. Arrange eggplant decoratively on cheese. Sprinkle with onion mixture, marjoram, dill, salt, pepper, and grated cheese.

Preheat oven, with pizza tile on lowest rack, to 425° F. Place pizza on tile and bake 20 minutes.

Pizza is done when crust is light golden brown and toppings are hot. Serve immediately.

Nutritional Data

PER SERVING		EXCHANGES	
Calories:	106	Milk:	0.0
Fat (gm):	3.1	Veg.:	0.0
Sat. fat (gm):	1.5	Fruit:	0.0
Cholesterol (mg):	8	Bread:	1.0
Sodium (mg):	155	Meat:	0.5
% Calories from fat:	26	Fat:	0.0

Goat's Cheese and Garlic Pizza

Goat's cheese is tangy yet light in texture. It blends well with sharper flavors.

12 Servings

(6 individual pizzas)

  1 Whole-Wheat Pizza Crust
     Canola oil, or non-stick cooking spray
  2 yellow peppers, seeded, sliced
  2 red peppers, seeded, sliced
 16 large garlic cloves, peeled, sliced horizontally
  6 ozs. plain goat's cheese, crumbled
 ½ teaspoon each: tarragon, caraway seeds

S hape and stretch dough by hand or with rolling pin on lightly floured pastry board. Divide into 6 individual pizzas, 6 or 7 inches each.

Preheat oven, with pizza tile or stone on lowest rack, to 435° F.

Oil or spray frying pan, and saute garlic and peppers a few minutes, until peppers begin to brown.

Cover pizzas with vegetables, goat's cheese, tarragon, and caraway seeds.

Using a pizza paddle lightly sprinkled with cornmeal, set pizzas one at time on pizza tile.

Bake 10 to 15 minutes or until pizza crust turns light golden brown. Remove pizzas from oven and cut each in half. Serve hot.

Nutritional Data

PER SERVING		EXCHANGES	
Calories:	175	Milk:	0.0
Fat (gm):	5.8	Veg.:	0.5
Sat. fat (gm):	2.9	Fruit:	0.0
Cholesterol (mg):	12	Bread:	1.5
Sodium (mg):	182	Meat:	0.5
% Calories from fat:	30	Fat:	0.5

CHEESE, PESTO, AND ASPARAGUS PIZZA

Break off the woody stems of asparagus spears before cooking. For a tender spear, you might want to peel the blunt end of each spear.

12 Servings

1 White or Yellow Cornmeal Pizza Crust (12-inch)
  Canola oil, or non-stick cooking spray
¾ cup pesto sauce
1 cup grated Alpine Lace low-cholesterol cheese
4 large cloves garlic, sliced horizontally
12 asparagus spears, trimmed, blanched
  Basil leaves, fresh, for garnish (if available)

Shape and stretch dough into a 12-inch circle or rectangle. Place dough on lightly oiled or sprayed pizza screen or pan.

Spread pesto sauce over crust. Sprinkle with cheese and garlic. Top with asparagus spears.

Prepare grill. When coals are hot, preheat pizza tile, about 10 minutes. Slide pizza onto tile or leave in pan or on screen.

Grill until pizza is done, about 5 to 10 minutes. Remove pizza with paddle and long-handled spatula. Place on serving dish; arrange fresh basil leaves on top. Serve hot.

(To cook this pizza in the oven, preheat oven to 425° F. Place pizza on tile on lowest oven rack and bake until done, about 20 minutes.)

Nutritional Data

PER SERVING		EXCHANGES	
Calories:	185	Milk:	0.0
Fat (gm):	5.5	Veg.:	0.0
Sat. fat (gm):	.6	Fruit:	0.0
Cholesterol (mg):	6	Bread:	1.5
Sodium (mg):	172	Meat:	1.0
% Calories from fat:	26	Fat:	0.5

PEAR AND BLUE CHEESE PIZZA

This pizza sounds very rich, but we use only a sprinkling of blue cheese to give a hint of flavor to the topping.

12 Servings

(6 individual pizzas)

- 1 Whole-Wheat Pizza Crust
  Canola oil, or non-stick cooking spray
- 1 tablespoon margarine
- 4 large, ripe but firm pears, cored, sliced thin
- 3 tablespoons lime juice, freshly squeezed
- ½ teaspoon ground cinnamon
- 1 oz. blue cheese, crumbled

S hape and stretch dough by hand or with rolling pin on lightly floured pastry board. Divide into 6 individual pizzas, 6 or 7 inches each.

Preheat oven to 425° F., with pizza tile on lowest rack.

Spray frying pan and melt margarine. Toss pear slices with lime juice and cinnamon. Saute pear slices only 1 minute.

Arrange pear slices on pizza. Sprinkle with blue cheese.

Using a pizza paddle lightly sprinkled with cornmeal, set pizzas one at a time on pizza tile.

Bake about 10 to 15 minutes or until pizza crusts turn light golden brown. Remove pizzas from oven and cut each in half. Serve hot.

Nutritional Data

PER SERVING		EXCHANGES	
Calories:	159	Milk:	0.0
Fat (gm):	2.8	Veg.:	0.0
Sat. fat (gm):	.7	Fruit:	0.5
Cholesterol (mg):	2	Bread:	1.5
Sodium (mg):	133	Meat:	0.0
% Calories from fat:	16	Fat:	0.5

CHEESE, ROASTED GARLIC, AND BASIL PIZZA

To roast the garlic, peel and cover lightly in aluminum foil. Roast garlic at 425° F. for 1 hour or until tender. Roasted garlic is good with any number of foods, for example, roast chicken or mashed potatoes. Usually roasted garlic is stored in olive oil, but we have eliminated that step.

12 Servings
1 Basic Pizza Crust (12-inch)
   Canola oil, or non-stick cooking spray
1½ cups non-fat Alpine lace cheese, grated
6 very large cloves garlic, or use elephant garlic, peeled, roasted, cooled, and sliced
½ cup fresh basil leaves, trimmed, washed, patted dry
1 teaspoon sesame seeds

S hape and stretch dough by hand or with rolling pin on lightly floured pastry board into 9 x 12-inch coated pan.

Preheat oven, with pizza tile on lowest rack, to 425° F.

Sprinkle cheese over crust. Arrange roasted garlic and basil on top of cheese. Sprinkle sesame seeds over pizza.

Place pizza on tile and bake 20 minutes. Pizza is done when crust is light golden brown and topping is hot. Serve immediately.

Nutritional Data

PER SERVING		EXCHANGES	
Calories:	104	Milk:	0.0
Fat (gm):	.7	Veg.:	0.0
Sat. fat (gm):	.0	Fruit:	0.0
Cholesterol (mg):	0	Bread:	1.0
Sodium (mg):	115	Meat:	1.0
% Calories from fat:	6	Fat:	0.0

MUSHROOM AND MADEIRA PIZZA

This pizza is for that special dressy occasion. It can easily be cut into small pieces and used as a first course. Chanterelle mushrooms have a milk-like, almost delicate taste while brown mushrooms have a richer, deeper taste.

12 Servings
1 Seeded Pizza Crust (12-inch)
  Canola oil, or non-stick cooking spray
2 tablespoons margarine
4 shallots, minced
3½ cups chanterelle and brown mushrooms, sliced
¼ cup Madeira wine
¼ teaspoon each: sage, white pepper
3 tablespoons chives, minced

Shape and stretch dough by hand or with rolling pin on lightly floured pastry board into 9 x 12-inch coated pan.

Preheat oven, with pizza tile on lowest rack, to 425° F.

Heat margarine in non-stick frying pan. Saute shallots until tender. Mix in mushrooms, and cook about 1 minute. Stir in Madeira wine and continue cooking until mushrooms are tender. Season with sage and pepper, and stir occasionally. Drain.

Spoon and spread mushroom mixture over crust, leaving a small rim around the pizza. Sprinkle chopped chives over top.

Place pizza on tile and bake 20 minutes. Pizza is done when crust is light golden brown and topping is hot. Serve immediately.

Nutritional Data

PER SERVING		EXCHANGES	
Calories:	77	Milk:	0.0
Fat (gm):	1.8	Veg.:	0.0
Sat. fat (gm):	.3	Fruit:	0.0
Cholesterol (mg):	0	Bread:	1.0
Sodium (mg):	68	Meat:	0.0
% Calories from fat:	21	Fat:	0.0

8.
PIZZA ON THE GRILL

$\boxed{A}$ t first thought, you might be doubtful about preparing pizza on the barbecue grill, but it is perfectly natural. The original pizzas, and some of the best made today, were cooked on wood-burning or tile stoves.

Innovations in pizza cooking utensils, such as the grill rack, have made pizza on the grill a breeze. It requires other special equipment: a pizza paddle, a long-handled spatula, and a pizza tray fitted with tiles. All the equipment is available at gourmet shops and most department stores. To make your own tile pizza tray, use a cookie sheet that is shaped to fit your grill, and set it with cooking tiles.

Take the pleasure of pizza outdoors to your grill for summer fun. Grilled pizza has a wonderful, savory, smoky flavor, and it is one of my favorites. Be sure to rotate pizzas during grilling so they cook evenly.

FAJITA PIZZA

*When grilling pizza, it makes sense to grill the toppings, too. Do it just minutes before arranging the pizza to grill.
Fajitas are strips of meat or chicken in a Southwest marinade, blended with peppers and onions. Fajitas are usually rolled in a tortilla, but we are using them as a pizza topping.*

12 Servings

Pizza
- 1 Basic Pizza Crust (12-inch)
   Canola oil, or non-stick cooking spray

Southwest Marinade
- 1½ cups light beer
- 2 tablespoons prepared mustard
- 5 tablespoons red wine vinegar
- 5 tablespoons dark brown sugar
- ½ teaspoon garlic powder

Fajitas
- 2 chicken breasts, skin discarded, bone removed
- 1 cup green bell pepper, sliced
- 1 cup onions, sliced in rounds, separated into rings
- 5 green onions, minced
- ½ cup cilantro, minced

Pizza: Stretch and shape dough by hand or use rolling pin on lightly floured board. Shape dough into 12-inch circle.

Marinade: Combine all marinade ingredients in saucepan. Simmer 4 minutes, stirring occasionally. Remove from heat; cool.

Fajitas: Cut chicken breasts into ½-inch strips. Marinate chicken in glass dish 45 minutes. Drain and reserve marinade.

Preheat grill. Spray grill screen with oil. Grill chicken strips, peppers, and onion rings over hot coals. Vegetables will cook in about 4 minutes; turn once. Brush vegetables with reserved marinade as they grill. Chicken cooks in about 6 minutes, turning once or twice.

Remove food from grill and arrange it on pizza crust, which may be placed on pizza screen, coated lightly with oil, or on paddle sprinkled lightly with cornmeal. Sprinkle pizza with green onions and cilantro.

While coals are hot, set pizza on tile. Cover and cook until pizza is done, about 5 to 6 minutes; crust will color slightly when pizza is finished. Using long-handle spatula, remove pizza onto paddle and place on serving dish. Bring to table hot.

Nutritional Data

PER SERVING		EXCHANGES	
Calories:	198	Milk:	0.0
Fat (gm):	2.5	Veg.:	1.0
Sat. fat (gm):	.5	Fruit:	0.0
Cholesterol (mg):	24	Bread:	1.5
Sodium (mg):	146	Meat:	1.0
% Calories from fat:	12	Fat:	0.0

TURKEY JALAPEÑO PIZZA ON FLATBREAD

If you are looking for a good recipe for leftover turkey, here it is.

12 Servings

2 cups plain non-fat yogurt
2 teaspoons lime rind, grated
2 cloves garlic, minced
4 green onions, minced
1 teaspoon ground cumin
¼ teaspoon white pepper
2 cups cooled turkey, chopped
6 pieces packaged Italian flatbread (about 4½ inch wide), or pita bread
3 jalapeño peppers, seeded, sliced (optional)

Spoon yogurt into a bowl. Mix in lime rind, garlic, onions, and spices. Add turkey and mix lightly.

Spread mixture over tops of flatbreads. Sprinkle with jalapeño peppers, to taste.

When coals are hot and pizza tile is preheated, begin grilling. Sprinkle small amount of cornmeal on pizza paddle, and slide pizza onto hot tile. Grill 5 minutes or until crusts and toppings are hot.

Using pizza paddle and long-handled spatula, move pizzas onto paddle, two at a time. Remove to serving dish. Cut each pizza in half. Serve hot.

Nutritional Data

PER SERVING		EXCHANGES	
Calories:	100	Milk:	0.5
Fat (gm):	.5	Veg.:	0.0
Sat. fat (gm):	.0	Fruit:	0.0
Cholesterol (mg):	16	Bread:	0.5
Sodium (mg):	202	Meat:	0.5
% Calories from fat:	5	Fat:	0.0

Mongolian Barbecue Pizza

◆

The food is barbecued on an indoor grill and then used as a topping for this tasty and different pizza. The indoor grill is a special cooking tool that is sold at most department stores and cookware shops.

◆

12 Servings

1 Whole-Wheat Pizza Crust (12-inch)
  Canola oil, or non-stick cooking spray
½ lb. chicken breast, boned, skinned
6 green onions, cut in half horizontally, then into 2-inch pieces
1 large red bell pepper, seeded, sliced
1 cup bean sprouts, blanched
½ cup bamboo shoots, sliced
3 garlic cloves, sliced
1 teaspoon ginger root, grated
1 teaspoon curry powder
3 tablespoons light soy sauce
¼ cup barbecue sauce (recipe follows)

Shape and stretch dough by hand or with rolling pin on lightly floured pastry board and fit into 9 x 12-inch sprayed pan.

Preheat oven, with pizza tile on lowest rack, to 425° F.

Meanwhile, preheat indoor grill according to manufacturer's directions (or use outdoor grill or skillet). Brush or spray grill with oil.

Grill chicken quickly on both sides until just barely cooked. Grill onions, sliced pepper, bean sprouts, and bamboo shoots until just grilled. Place all ingredients in deep bowl. Toss with garlic, ginger, curry powder, soy sauce, and Barbecue Sauce (recipe follows).

Arrange cooked ingredients over pizza crust.

Place pizza on tile and bake 20 minutes or until crust is light golden brown and topping is hot. Serve immediately.

BARBECUE SAUCE (Makes 1¾ cups)

Canola oil, or non-stick cooking spray
¾ cup onions, chopped
2 cloves garlic, minced
1½ cups tomatoes, crushed
3 tablespoons cider vinegar
3 tablespoons orange juice, freshly squeezed
3 tablespoons light brown sugar
1 teaspoon each: Worcestershire sauce, chili powder
½ teaspoon each: salt, celery seeds
¼ teaspoon each: Tabasco sauce, pepper

Spray saucepan with oil and saute onions and garlic until soft, stirring occasionally. Add remaining ingredients and simmer 10 minutes, stirring occasionally. Cool sauce. Place cooled sauce in covered container and refrigerate until needed.

Nutritional Data

PER SERVING		EXCHANGES	
Calories:	84	Milk:	0.0
Fat (gm):	1.1	Veg.:	1.0
Sat. fat (gm):	.2	Fruit:	0.0
Cholesterol (mg):	7	Bread:	1.0
Sodium (mg):	208	Meat:	0.0
% Calories from fat:	11	Fat:	0.0

THAI-FLAVORED PIZZA

A combination of traditional Thai flavors blended on the pizza crust. Soon to be a favorite.

12 Servings

1 Basic Pizza Crust (12-inch)
  Canola oil, or non-stick cooking spray
⅓ cup lime juice, freshly squeezed
¼ cup fish sauce (a Thai ingredient, now available at most large supermarkets)
¼ teaspoon ground red chili
1 teaspoon dark brown sugar
½ lb. flank steak, trimmed, visible fat removed
1 medium onion, cut into ¼- to ½-inch slices
1 cup green bell pepper, sliced
1 cup cucumber, peeled, sliced
½ cup cilantro, chopped

P repare crust according to basic recipe. Knead and stretch dough to fit oiled 9 x 12-inch pan.

Combine lime juice, fish sauce, chili, and sugar. Brush meat on both sides. Reserve extra sauce.

Prepare grill. When coals are hot, cook steak until medium, turning as needed and brushing with sauce. Reserve any remaining sauce.

At the same time you are grilling the steak, grill the onions until slightly charred. Separate onion into rings.

Remove steak from grill and cut against the grain into thin pieces.

Arrange meat on pizza crust. Distribute onion rings, pepper slices, cucumber, and cilantro over top of pizza. Sprinkle pizza with reserved sauce.

Preheat pizza tile on grill, about 10 minutes. When hot, slide pizza onto tile, using pizza paddle lightly dusted with cornmeal.

Cover and cook until pizza is done, about 5 to 6 minutes. Crust will be cooked when light golden brown. Slide pizza onto paddle, using long-handled spatula, and place on serving dish. Cut pizza into 12 pieces, and bring to the table hot.

Nutritional Data

PER SERVING		EXCHANGES	
Calories:	170	Milk:	0.0
Fat (gm):	3.5	Veg.:	0.5
Sat. fat (gm):	1.0	Fruit:	0.0
Cholesterol (mg):	13	Bread:	1.5
Sodium (mg):	148	Meat:	1.0
% Calories from fat:	19	Fat:	0.0

Eggplant and Basil Pizza

If at all possible, have an herb garden. The best place to locate it is outside the kitchen door, as they do in France. But even a flower pot in the kitchen can be very rewarding. Garnish this pizza with fresh basil leaves, if available.

12 Servings

1 large, well-formed eggplant, about 1½ lbs., trimmed, sliced in rounds ¼ to ½ inch thick
2 tablespoons margarine
3 cloves garlic, minced
1½ cups onions, chopped
2 teaspoons curry powder
½ teaspoon ground cinnamon
½ teaspoon basil, chopped
¼ teaspoon each: salt, pepper
1 Whole-Wheat Pizza Crust (12-inch)
2 tablespoons anise seeds
Canola oil, or non-stick cooking spray
Fresh basil leaves for garnish, optional

Drain eggplant. Sprinkle slices with salt. Let stand 20 minutes on paper towels. Wash eggplant slices to remove salt, and pat dry with paper towels. Cut eggplant into ¼-inch cubes.

Heat margarine in non-stick frying pan, add garlic and onions, and cook over medium heat until soft. Add eggplant and saute until tender, stirring occasionally. Season with curry powder, cinnamon, basil, salt, and pepper.

Prepare dough. When kneading, mix in anise seeds. Shape and stretch dough into oiled 12 x 9-inch rectangular pan (or leave dough free-form).

Spread cooled eggplant mixture evenly over crust.

Prepare grill. When coals are hot, preheat pizza tile, about 10 minutes. Slide pizza onto tile, using pizza paddle sprinkled lightly with cornmeal.

Grill until pizza is done, about 5 to 10 minutes. Again, slide pizza onto paddle and bring it to serving dish. Garnish pizza with fresh basil leaves. Bring to table hot.

Nutritional Data

PER SERVING		EXCHANGES	
Calories:	89	Milk:	0.0
Fat (gm):	2.0	Veg.:	0.5
Sat. fat (gm):	.3	Fruit:	0.0
Cholesterol (mg):	0	Bread:	1.0
Sodium (mg):	113	Meat:	0.0
% Calories from fat:	19	Fat:	0.0

EGGPLANT MIDDLE EASTERN PIZZA ON PITA

The Griffo pizza rack is a very useful tool that can be used both indoors and on the grill. The pizza rack is placed directly on the grill or tile. It helps circulate air, giving you a better, crispier crust.

12 Servings

1 large eggplant (about 7 to 8 inches long), cut in half
1 large bell pepper
  Canola oil, or non-stick cooking spray
3 cloves garlic, minced
1 large tomato, peeled, seeded, chopped
1 tablespoon good quality olive oil
2 tablespoons lemon or lime juice, freshly squeezed
¾ teaspoon ground cumin
¼ teaspoon each: salt, ground black pepper, celery seeds
6 whole pita breads, separated into halves (see next recipe, or use store-bought pitas)

When coals are hot, set eggplant halves and whole bell pepper on sprayed grill rack. Grill, turning occasionally, until eggplant is tender, about 10 minutes. Grill pepper until charred on all sides, 4 to 6 minutes.

Using a fork, remove pepper from grill, put in plastic bag and let stand 10 minutes. Remove pepper from bag. Peel pepper and discard seeds. Spoon out eggplant flesh, discarding seeds.

Using food processor fitted with steel blade, mince garlic and tomato. Add eggplant, pepper, and remaining ingredients, except pitas. Puree.

Spread eggplant mixture on pita breads.

Preheat pizza tile, about 10 minutes. Set pita breads on hot tile. Grill uncovered 5 to 6 minutes.

With pizza paddle and long-handled spatula, move pizzas onto paddle, about two at a time. Serve hot.

Nutritional Data

PER SERVING		EXCHANGES	
Calories:	79	Milk:	0.0
Fat (gm):	1.5	Veg.:	0.0
Sat. fat (gm):	.2	Fruit:	0.0
Cholesterol (mg):	0	Bread:	1.0
Sodium (mg):	154	Meat:	0.0
% Calories from fat:	17	Fat:	0.0

EGGPLANT, BLACK OLIVE, AND CHEESE PIZZA

Small black Greek olives may be substituted for canned olives. They are as delicious but high in sodium.

12 Servings

1 large, well-formed eggplant (about 1½ lbs.), trimmed, sliced into ¼-inch rounds, unpeeled
1 tablespoon good quality olive oil
4 garlic cloves, minced
1 Basic Pizza Crust (12-inch)
2 tablespoons celery seeds
  Canola oil, or non-stick cooking spray
¼ cup black olives, sliced, drained
1 cup low-cholesterol Alpine Lace cheese, shredded
¾ teaspoon tarragon
¼ teaspoon each: salt, ground black pepper

S prinkle eggplant slices with salt to remove moisture. Let stand 20 minutes on paper towels. Rinse eggplant slices and pat dry with paper towels.

Heat olive oil and garlic in large frying pan over medium heat. Saute eggplant, covered, gently about 2 minutes on each side. Eggplant will be cooked when golden brown and soft.

Prepare dough according to basic recipe; when kneading, mix in celery seeds. Use a rolling pin or knead dough by hand on lightly floured board. Shape dough into 12-inch pizza pan that has been lightly oiled or sprayed with non-stick cooking spray.

Arrange eggplant pieces with garlic decoratively on pizza crust. Sprinkle on black olives, cheese, and seasonings.

Preheat grill. When coals are hot, preheat tiles.

Slide pizza onto tiles, using pizza paddle sprinkled lightly with cornmeal.

Cook until pizza is done, about 5 to 6 minutes, or until done to taste. It might be necessary to rotate pizza during grilling. Using long-handled spatula, remove pizza to serving dish. Slice and bring to table hot.

Nutritional Data

PER SERVING		EXCHANGES	
Calories:	157	Milk:	0.0
Fat (gm):	3.8	Veg.:	1.0
Sat. fat (gm):	.7	Fruit:	0.0
Cholesterol (mg):	1	Bread:	1.5
Sodium (mg):	179	Meat:	0.0
% Calories from fat:	22	Fat:	0.5

SPINACH, RAISIN, AND GINGERED WALNUT PIZZA

This recipe is from the talented Don Hysho of Peoples Smoke & Grill Company, Cumberland, Rhode Island.

12 Servings
6 ozs. pizza dough
Canola oil, or non-stick cooking spray
1 tablespoon virgin olive oil (divided)
½ teaspoon garlic, minced
½ cup low-fat Alpine Lace cheese, shredded
4 tablespoons chopped canned tomatoes in heavy puree
8 to 10 fresh, tender spinach leaves, washed, patted dry
1 tablespoon raisins
1 tablespoon chopped walnuts on which freshly grated ginger has been placed

1. Prepare hot charwood (charcoal) fire, setting grill rack 3 to 4 inches above coals.
2. On a large, oiled or sprayed inverted baking sheet, spread and flatten pizza dough with your hands into 10 to 12-inch free-form circle, ⅛ inch thick. Do not make a lip. Maintain even thickness.
3. When fire is hot (when you can hold your hand over coals 3 to 4 seconds at a distance of 5 inches), use fingertips to lift dough gently by the two corners closest to you, and place it on grill. Catch loose edges on the grill first, and guide remaining dough into place over fire. Within a minute, dough will puff slightly, underside will be stiff, and grill marks will appear.
4. Using tongs, immediately flip crust over, onto coolest part of grill, or use pizza tile or pizza rack. Quickly brush grill surface with ½ tablespoon olive oil. Scatter garlic and cheese over dough, and spoon dollops of tomatoes over the cheese. Do not cover entire surface of pizza with tomatoes. Finally, drizzle pizza with remaining ½ tablespoon olive oil and top with spinach, raisins, and walnuts with grated ginger.
5. Slide pizza back toward hot coals but not directly over them. Using tongs, rotate pizza frequently so that different sections receive high heat. Check underside often to see that it is not burning. Pizza is done when top is bubbly and cheese melted, about 6 to 8 minutes. Serve at once.

Nutritional Data

PER SERVING		EXCHANGES	
Calories:	53	Milk:	0.0
Fat (gm):	1.8	Veg.:	0.0
Sat. fat (gm):	.1	Fruit:	0.0
Cholesterol (mg):	0	Bread:	0.5
Sodium (mg):	44	Meat:	0.5
% Calories from fat:	30	Fat:	0.0

TOMATILLO AND CLAM PIZZA

Tomatillos resemble green tomatoes in looks. It is a Mexican vegetable, having an outer husk that is removed before cooking. Available in Mexican grocery stores and at large supermarkets.

14 Servings

- 1 tablespoon good quality olive oil
- 1 lb. tomatillos, washed, husks discarded. Blanch until skin begins to separate. Remove skins and chop.
- 1 cup red onions, sliced
- ½ cup celery, sliced
- ¼ cup cilantro, chopped
- ½ teaspoon celery seeds
- ¼ teaspoon each: ground coriander, salt, pepper
    Canola oil, or non-stick cooking spray
- 7 English muffins, split
- 1 can (7½ ounces) minced clams

Heat oil in large frying pan. Saute tomatillos, onion, and celery over medium heat, stirring occasionally, until vegetables are tender. Mix in cilantro, celery seeds, coriander, salt, and pepper.

Preheat grill. When coals are hot, put sprayed grill rack on grid.

Toast muffins, cut side down, just until lightly toasted. Remove muffins and spread with tomatillo sauce. Top muffins with drained clams.

Return muffins to grill rack and grill only to warm the muffins. Serve muffins hot.

Nutritional Data

PER SERVING		EXCHANGES	
Calories:	104	Milk:	0.0
Fat (gm):	1.8	Veg.:	0.0
Sat. fat (gm):	.2	Fruit:	0.0
Cholesterol (mg):	9	Bread:	1.0
Sodium (mg):	238	Meat:	0.5
% Calories from fat:	16	Fat:	0.0

MANDARIN ORANGE AND ONION PIZZA

◆

This recipe is an adaptation of a classic Mexican salad.

◆

12 Servings

(6 individual pizzas)

1 Whole-Wheat Pizza Crust
3 tablespoons cilantro, minced (divided)
2 tablespoons margarine
2 cups red onions, sliced
½ teaspoon salt
½ teaspoon ground cumin
¼ teaspoon pepper
1 can (10¾ ounces) mandarin oranges, drained
⅓ cup toasted walnuts

While kneading dough, mix in 2 tablespoons minced cilantro. Divide dough into 6 pieces. Shape and stretch dough by hand or roll out on slightly floured pastry cloth into 6 approximately 6-inch circles or squares.

Heat margarine in frying pan. Saute onions 4 minutes over medium heat. Season with salt, cumin, and pepper. Cool.

Spread onion mixture over pizza. Sprinkle with mandarin oranges, walnuts, and remaining cilantro.

Preheat grill. When coals are hot, preheat tiles.

Sprinkle small amount of cornmeal on pizza paddle, and slide pizzas onto hot tiles. Cover grill and cook about 5 to 6 minutes or until pizza crusts are firm and toppings hot.

Using pizza paddle and long-handled spatula, remove pizzas and bring to table hot. Cut pizzas in half before serving.

Nutritional Data

PER SERVING		EXCHANGES	
Calories:	164	Milk:	0.0
Fat (gm):	4.6	Veg.:	0.5
Sat. fat (gm):	.4	Fruit:	0.0
Cholesterol (mg):	0	Bread:	1.5
Sodium (mg):	181	Meat:	0.0
% Calories from fat:	25	Fat:	0.5

Tomato-Orange Sauce and Artichoke Pizza

This sauce works well with spaghetti as well as pizza.

---

12 Servings

Tomato Sauce
  - 1 tablespoon good quality olive oil
  - 3 cloves garlic, minced
  - ½ cup onions, chopped
  - 1 can (28 ounces) crushed tomatoes with liquid
  - 2 tablespoons catsup
  - 2 tablespoons orange juice, freshly squeezed
  - 1 tablespoon orange rind
  - ½ teaspoon each: oregano, basil, pepper

Pizza
  - 1 Whole-Wheat Pizza Crust (12-inch)
     Canola oil, or non-stick cooking spray
  - 2 tablespoons fennel seeds
  - 1 jar (4½ ounces) artichokes, drained

Tomato Sauce: Heat olive oil in non-stick saucepan over medium heat. Saute garlic and onions, covered, about 3 minutes, stirring occasionally. Mix in tomatoes with liquid, catsup, juice, rind, oregano, basil, and pepper. Reduce heat to simmer, and continue cooking 20 minutes, uncovered, stirring occasionally. Cool.

Pizza: Shape and stretch dough into 12-inch circle or rectangle and place on oiled pan or pizza screen. Sprinkle fennel seeds over crust.

Spread tomato-orange sauce over crust. Quarter the drained artichokes and sprinkle over sauce.

Prepare grill. When coals are hot and pizza tile is preheated, begin grilling. Place pizza on grill using paddle sprinkled lightly with cornmeal, or leave pizza on grill rack and set directly over tiles. Grill about 5 to 10 minutes or until pizza is cooked. Crust will be hot and beginning to color and topping will be hot.

With pizza paddle and long-handled spatula, move pizza onto paddle. Bring to table, cut into pieces, and serve hot.

Nutritional Data

PER SERVING		EXCHANGES	
Calories:	85	Milk:	0.0
Fat (gm):	1.8	Veg.:	0.5
Sat. fat (gm):	.2	Fruit:	0.0
Cholesterol (mg):	0	Bread:	1.0
Sodium (mg):	165	Meat:	0.0
% Calories from fat:	18	Fat:	0.0

Ratatouille Pizza

Usually ratatouille is a stew made of vegetables, but here we use the vegetables, grilled individually and cooked on a cilantro-whole-wheat pizza crust, to create the same wonderful flavor.
A Griffo Grill is a very important grilling tool, available at hardware stores, department stores, and specialty shops throughout the country. The Griffo Grill is a screen that fits directly over your grill, preventing small pieces of food from falling through the grid onto the hot coals.

24 Servings

Pizza

  2 Whole-Wheat Pizza Crusts (12-inch)
  ½ cup cilantro, minced
    Canola oil, or non-stick cooking spray

Provence Brushing Sauce

  2 tablespoons olive oil
  ¼ cup lemon juice, freshly squeezed
  ½ teaspoon each: thyme, sage

Vegetables

  1 eggplant, about 1 lb., peeled, sliced
    horizontally in ½-inch-thick pieces
    Canola oil, or non-stick cooking spray
  2 cups zucchini, sliced
  1½ cups green bell peppers, seeded, sliced
  1 large onion, cut into ½-inch rounds, left whole
  1½ cups tomatoes, sliced
  1 cup parsley, minced

Pizza: When kneading dough, mix in cilantro. Use rolling pin or knead dough by hand on lightly floured board. Shape and stretch dough into 2, 12-inch coated pizza pans or 9 x 12-inch rectangular pans. Or shape pizzas free form and use a sprayed pizza rack.

Brushing Sauce: Mix all ingredients together in small bowl. Set aside.

Vegetables: Sprinkle eggplant slices with salt. Let drain on paper towels 30 minutes. Wash off all salt and pat eggplant dry.

Prepare grill. When coals are hot, set sprayed grill screen in place over grate. Brush all vegetables with sauce, and grill about 2 minutes on each side or until vegetables are beginning to char and get tender. Eggplant slices will take a little longer. Grill until vegetables are cooked, brushing with sauce as you turn or as needed. Sprinkle with parsley.

Arrange vegetables on pizza crust, which may be placed on a pizza screen coated lightly with oil, or on a paddle sprinkled lightly with cornmeal.

While coals are hot, set pizza on preheated tile. Cover and cook until pizza is done, about 5 to 6 minutes; crust will color slightly when pizza is finished. Using long-handle spatula, remove pizza onto paddle and place on serving dish. Bring to table hot.

Nutritional Data

PER SERVING		EXCHANGES	
Calories:	81	Milk:	0.0
Fat (gm):	2.0	Veg.:	0.5
Sat. fat (gm):	.3	Fruit:	0.0
Cholesterol (mg):	0	Bread:	1.0
Sodium (mg):	115	Meat:	0.0
% Calories from fat:	21	Fat:	0.0

VEGETARIAN PIZZA

The vegetables in this pizza are chosen to be complimentary to each other. The festive colors of the vegetables make a lovely presentation.

12 Servings

1 Whole-Wheat Pizza Crust (12-inch)
  Canola oil, or non-stick cooking spray
2 tablespoons margarine
1 cup zucchini, thinly sliced
1 cup onions, chopped
1 cup celery, chopped
1 cup broccoli florets
1 teaspoon each: oregano, basil, grated lemon peel, parsley
¾ cup low-cholesterol Cheddar cheese, grated

To prepare dough, shape and stretch it into 12-inch circle or rectangle. Place it on a paddle, sprinkled lightly with cornmeal, or on oiled pizza screen.

Heat margarine in large frying pan over medium heat. Saute zucchini, onions, celery, and broccoli about 5 minutes, stirring occasionally until tender. Season with oregano, basil, lemon peel, and parsley.

Arrange vegetables over crust. Sprinkle pizza with cheese.

Prepare grill. When coals are hot, preheat pizza tile about 10 minutes. Slide pizza onto tile.

Grill until pizza is done, about 5 to 10 minutes; crust will be light golden color and vegetables tender. When cooked, again slide pizza onto paddle and set it on serving dish.

Nutritional Data

PER SERVING		EXCHANGES	
Calories:	110	Milk:	0.0
Fat (gm):	3.2	Veg.:	0.5
Sat. fat (gm):	.3	Fruit:	0.0
Cholesterol (mg):	5	Bread:	1.0
Sodium (mg):	103	Meat:	0.5
% Calories from fat:	26	Fat:	0.0

SALSA PIZZA

My salsa-loving daughter, Dorothy, was the inspiration for using salsa ingredients as a topping on this pizza.

12 Servings
1 Whole-Wheat Pizza Crust (12-inch)
2 tablespoons cumin seeds
  Canola oil, or non-stick cooking spray
1 tablespoon good quality olive oil
1½ cups onions, sliced
¼ teaspoon each: salt, pepper, garlic powder
3 tomatoes, thinly sliced
6 cloves garlic, sliced horizontally
2 jalapeño peppers, seeded, thinly sliced

While kneading dough, mix in cumin seeds. If dough is too sticky, add more flour, 2 tablespoons at a time. Shape and stretch dough on a lightly floured board until large enough to fit into coated pizza pan.

Heat olive oil in non-stick frying pan over medium heat. Saute onions until tender, about 4 minutes. Season with salt, pepper, and garlic powder.

Arrange tomatoes over pizza, and top with sliced garlic, onion mixture, and Jalapeño peppers.

Preheat grill. When coals are hot, preheat tiles.

Sprinkle small amount of cornmeal on pizza paddle. Slide pizza onto hot tiles. Cook until pizza is done, 5 to 6 minutes. Crust will be firm, hot, and beginning to color; and toppings will be hot.

Using long-handled spatula, slide pizza onto paddle and place on serving dish. Bring to table hot.

Nutritional Data

PER SERVING		EXCHANGES	
Calories:	85	Milk:	0.0
Fat (gm):	2.2	Veg.:	0.0
Sat. fat (gm):	.3	Fruit:	0.0
Cholesterol (mg):	0	Bread:	1.0
Sodium (mg):	98	Meat:	0.0
% Calories from fat:	23	Fat:	0.5

Salsa and Cheese Pizza

Don't be fooled. Always wear rubber gloves when working with jalapeño peppers to protect your eyes and skin from their strong oils.

---

6 Servings

Salsa

- 1½ cups green bell peppers, seeded, chopped
- 2 jalapeño peppers, seeded, chopped
- 3 tomatoes, peeled, seeded, chopped
- 1 cup onions, minced
- ¾ cup cilantro, chopped
- 3 tablespoons fresh lime or lemon juice
- 4 cloves garlic, minced
- ¼ teaspoon pepper

Pizza

- 3 pieces packaged Italian flatbread (about 4½ inches wide)
- 2 cups white mushrooms, sliced
- ½ cup non-fat cheese, shredded

Salsa: Prepare by tossing all salsa ingredients together in a deep bowl. Cover lightly and chill until ready to use. Mix before using.

Pizza: Spoon salsa on flatbread. Spread with back of spoon. Sprinkle with mushrooms and top with cheese.

Preheat grill. When coals are hot, preheat tile.

Sprinkle a small amount of cornmeal on pizza paddle. Slide pizzas onto hot tile. Cook 5 to 6 minutes or until crusts and toppings are hot, the cheese melted.

Using a long-handled spatula, slide pizzas off tiles and onto pizza paddle. Place pizzas on serving dish and cut each in half. Bring to the table hot.

Nutritional Data

PER SERVING		EXCHANGES	
Calories:	117	Milk:	0.0
Fat (gm):	.9	Veg.:	1.0
Sat. fat (gm):	.0	Fruit:	0.0
Cholesterol (mg):	0	Bread:	0.5
Sodium (mg):	156	Meat:	1.0
% Calories from fat:	7	Fat:	0.0

Mango Salsa Pizza

Also try honeydew or cantaloupe in place of mango.

12 Servings

(6 individual pizzas)

Pizza
- 1 Basic Pizza Crust (12-inch)
- 2 tablespoons dried cilantro

Mango Salsa
- ½ cup cilantro, minced
- 1–2 cups red or green bell peppers, seeded, chopped
- ½ cup each: minced onions, minced mango, chopped fresh pineapple
- 1 tablespoon lime juice, freshly squeezed

Pizza: Prepare dough according to basic recipe. While kneading dough, mix in cilantro. Divide dough into 6 pieces.

Shape and stretch dough by hand or roll out on slightly floured pastry cloth into 6 approximately 6-inch squares or triangles.

Mango Salsa: Toss cilantro, peppers, onions, mango, pineapple, and lime juice in deep bowl. Cover lightly and chill until ready to use. Mix and drain salsa before using.

Spoon salsa over crust, using back of spoon to spread it evenly.

Prepare grill. When coals are hot and pizza tile is preheated, begin grilling. Sprinkle small amount of cornmeal on pizza paddle. Slide pizza onto hot tile. Cook about 5 to 10 minutes or until pizza crust is light golden color and topping is hot.

With pizza paddle and long-handled spatula, move pizza onto paddle and bring to table hot. Cut pizzas in half before serving.

Nutritional Data

PER SERVING		EXCHANGES	
Calories:	135	Milk:	0.0
Fat (gm):	1.5	Veg.:	0.0
Sat. fat (gm):	.2	Fruit:	0.5
Cholesterol (mg):	0	Bread:	1.5
Sodium (mg):	90	Meat:	0.0
% Calories from fat:	10	Fat:	0.0

CHEESE, PESTO, AND ASPARAGUS PIZZA

Break off the woody asparagus stems before cooking. For a tender spear, you might want to peel the remaining end of each spear.

12 Servings

- 1 White or Yellow Cornmeal Pizza Crust (12-inch)
  Canola oil, or non-stick cooking spray
- ¾ cup pesto sauce
- 1 cup Alpine Lace low-cholesterol cheese, grated
- 4 large cloves garlic, sliced horizontally
- 12 asparagus spears, trimmed, blanched
  Fresh basil leaves for garnish, if available

Prepare dough. Shape and stretch dough into 12-inch circle or rectangle. Place on lightly oiled pizza screen or pan.

Spread pesto sauce over crust. Sprinkle crust with cheese and garlic. Arrange asparagus spears decoratively over crust.

Prepare grill. When coals are hot, preheat pizza tile, about 10 minutes. Slide pizza onto tile or leave on screen.

Grill until pizza is done, about 5 to 10 minutes. Remove pizza with paddle and long-handled spatula. Place on serving dish; arrange fresh basil leaves on top. Serve hot.

Nutritional Data

PER SERVING		EXCHANGES	
Calories:	185	Milk:	0.0
Fat (gm):	5.5	Veg.:	0.0
Sat. fat (gm):	.6	Fruit:	0.0
Cholesterol (mg):	6	Bread:	1.5
Sodium (mg):	172	Meat:	1.0
% Calories from fat:	26	Fat:	0.5

WHOLE-WHEAT PITA BREAD

Pita bread is a Middle Eastern bread, flat and round in shape, and hollow inside. It is usually cut in half to form a pocket. For pizza, the pita is separated into two pieces of bread.

12 Servings

(6 individual pitas)

½ teaspoon honey
1 cup warm water, about 110° F.
1 package active dry yeast
2 tablespoons good quality olive oil
1 cup whole-wheat flour
2 cups all-purpose flour
½ teaspoon salt

To proof yeast, stir honey into warm water, using measuring cup or small bowl. Sprinkle yeast over water and stir until yeast dissolves. Let mixture stand in draft-free area about 5 minutes or until yeast begins to bubble.

Mix in olive oil. In food processor fitted with steel blade or in electric mixer with dough hook, mix flours with salt. Add yeast mixture to flour and process until soft, almost sticky dough is formed, about 5 to 10 seconds. If using an electric mixer, blend 5 to 8 minutes or until smooth dough is formed. If mixing dough by hand, on lightly floured surface or pastry cloth, mix about 5 minutes or until dough is smooth. Add flour by the tablespoon if dough is too sticky.

Let dough rise in bowl covered with aluminum foil. Set bowl in warm, draft-free area about 1 hour or until dough bubbles.

Punch dough down.

Turn dough out on lightly floured board. Divide into 6 pieces. Roll dough into balls. Cover and set aside 25 to 30 minutes.

Using rolling pin covered with pastry sleeve, roll each piece of dough into 8-inch circle. Sprinkle a handful of cornmeal on cookie sheet. Set rolled dough on cookie sheet and let stand 25 to 30 minutes.

Preheat oven to 500° F. Bake breads on lowest oven rack 5 minutes. Reduce heat to 350° F. Move cookie sheet to middle of oven and continue baking 5 minutes. Breads will puff and just begin to color. Remove breads from oven and cool on rack. Cover cooled breads and refrigerate or freeze.

Nutritional Data

PER SERVING		EXCHANGES	
Calories:	132	Milk:	0.0
Fat (gm):	2.6	Veg.:	0.0
Sat. fat (gm):	.4	Fruit:	0.0
Cholesterol (mg):	0	Bread:	1.5
Sodium (mg):	89	Meat:	0.0
% Calories from fat:	18	Fat:	0.5

9.
SPECIALTY PIZZAS

I have included some specialty crusts in various recipes throughout this book, but this chapter will be exclusively dedicated to them. Specialty crusts make an interesting, tasty, and often lighter variation on traditional crusts. Some representative specialty crusts are Boboli bread, which has a cheesy flavor, English muffins for individual mini pizzas, large Middle Eastern lahvosh crackers, and packaged pizza dough from your supermarket's dairy case.

Specialty crusts add flair to a pizza party and create an unusual and innovative touch.

CREOLE PIZZA

A taste of New Orleans is fine on a pizza. The Creole sauce adds a spicy and flavorful component.

15 Servings
- 1 can (16 ounces) crushed tomatoes, with liquid
- ¾ cup celery, finely chopped
- ¾ cup red bell pepper, finely chopped
- ½ cup onions, finely chopped
- 3 tablespoons sweet pickle relish
- 1 lb. large shrimp, peeled, deveined
- ¼ teaspoon each: salt, pepper, marjoram
- 1 package pizza dough, in dairy case of supermarket

Pour crushed tomatoes into saucepan. Stir in celery, bell pepper, onions, and relish. Bring sauce to a boil. Reduce heat to simmer, and cook uncovered 15 minutes, stirring occasionally.

Mix in shrimp, salt, pepper, marjoram. Continue cooking 5 minutes. Cool.

Unroll dough. Stretch and press dough into lightly oiled or non-stick cookie sheet, or 15 x 10-inch rectangular pan.

Spoon cooled Creole sauce over pizza.

Bake pizza on lowest rack of oven 10 to 15 minutes or until crust begins to color.

Cut into squares. Serve hot.

Nutritional Data

PER SERVING		EXCHANGES	
Calories:	85	Milk:	0.0
Fat (gm):	.9	Veg.:	1.0
Sat. fat (gm):	.1	Fruit:	0.0
Cholesterol (mg):	46	Bread:	0.5
Sodium (mg):	259	Meat:	0.5
% Calories from fat:	10	Fat:	0.0

NACHO PIZZA

For a fiesta or party first course, try fruit gazpacho. Follow with this nacho pizza, and serve colorful fresh fruit for dessert.

12 Servings
1 loaf frozen bread dough, defrosted
2 tablespoons cumin seeds
  Canola oil, or non-stick cooking spray
2 tablespoons margarine
1½ cups onions, chopped
1 cup green bell peppers, chopped
½ teaspoon each: garlic powder, chili powder
6 ozs. non-fat cheese, grated
3 jalapeño chilies, seeded, sliced

Tear dough into 6 equal pieces. Roll each piece of dough into 6- to 7-inch circles or squares. Sprinkle with cumin seeds. Set aside on sprayed grill rack, or you may cook directly on preheated pizza tile.

Heat margarine in frying pan over medium heat. Saute onions and peppers 3 minutes, stirring occasionally. Season with garlic powder and chili powder.

Spread vegetables over pizzas. Sprinkle with cheese and jalapeño peppers.

Nutritional Data

PER SERVING		EXCHANGES	
Calories:	138	Milk:	0.0
Fat (gm):	3.9	Veg.:	0.5
Sat. fat (gm):	.2	Fruit:	0.0
Cholesterol (mg):	0	Bread:	1.0
Sodium (mg):	299	Meat:	0.5
% Calories from fat:	25	Fat:	1.0

Szechwan Chicken Pizza

Once again we are borrowing tastes and combinations from Chinese cuisine. Adjust hot spices to taste.

15 Servings

1	egg white, slightly beaten
¼	cup white wine
2	tablespoons cornstarch
1	cup chicken breasts, boned, skin discarded, cut into thin strips
1	tablespoon canola oil
4	green onions, minced
2	teaspoons fresh ginger root, grated
2	cloves garlic, minced
1	cup each, chopped: celery, green bell pepper
3	tablespoons catsup
½	teaspoon red pepper flakes
¼	teaspoon salt
¼	cup chicken stock
1½	teaspoons cornstarch, mixed with 2 tablespoons water
1	package pizza dough in dairy case at supermarket
	Canola oil non-stick spray

In a bowl, combine egg white, wine, and cornstarch. Add chicken strips to mixture and let marinate 1 hour at room temperature.

Heat 1 tablespoon oil in wok or large frying pan. Stir-fry onions, ginger, and garlic 30 seconds. Add chicken mixture and stir-fry until just cooked.

Add celery and bell pepper and stir-fry 1 minute longer. Add remaining ingredients and stir-fry until mixture thickens slightly.

Preheat oven to 425° F.

Unroll dough. Stretch and press dough into lightly oiled or non-stick cookie sheet, 15 x 10-inch rectangular shape. Spread Szechwan chicken mixture over crust.

Bake pizza on lowest rack 10 to 15 minutes or until crust is cooked and topping hot.

Nutritional Data

PER SERVING		EXCHANGES	
Calories:	84	Milk:	0.0
Fat (gm):	1.8	Veg.:	0.0
Sat. fat (gm):	.2	Fruit:	0.0
Cholesterol (mg):	6	Bread:	1.0
Sodium (mg):	191	Meat:	0.5
% Calories from fat:	20	Fat:	0.0

HOISIN CHICKEN PIZZA

Hoisin sauce is a wonderful, dark, rich bean sauce available at oriental food stores and large supermarkets.

15 Servings

1 package pizza dough, in dairy case at supermarket
  Canola oil, or non-stick cooking spray
1 tablespoon canola oil
2 cups green onions, chopped (divided)
1 teaspoon ginger, grated
1 tablespoon garlic, grated
1 cup snow peas, trimmed, chopped
2 cups chicken breast, chopped
¼ cup Hoisin sauce
¼ cup chicken stock
¼ teaspoon each: salt, pepper

Unroll dough. Stretch and press dough into lightly oiled non-stick cookie sheet, 15 x 10-inch rectangular shape.

Heat oil in wok or non-stick frying pan. Stir-fry green onions, garlic, and ginger 1 minute. Add snow peas.

Mix in chicken. Stir-fry until chicken just loses its color. Blend in Hoisin sauce and chicken stock.

Season with salt and pepper. Cook 1 minute more or until sauce thickens slightly.

Spread chicken mixture over crust.

Preheat oven, with tile on lowest rack, to 425° F. Bake pizza on lowest rack 10 to 15 minutes or until crust begins to color.

Nutritional Data

PER SERVING		EXCHANGES	
Calories:	93	Milk:	0.0
Fat (gm):	2.1	Veg.:	0.0
Sat. fat (gm):	.2	Fruit:	0.0
Cholesterol (mg):	13	Bread:	1.0
Sodium (mg):	163	Meat:	0.5
% Calories from fat:	20	Fat:	0.0

SMOKED TURKEY PIZZA

You can use leftover turkey or chicken for this recipe, but for a real treat, try smoking the poultry. (Always use hardwood charcoal for best results.)

16 Servings

Smoked Turkey

1 turkey breast (about 3½ lbs.) washed, patted dry, fat discarded

3 pieces mesquite or hickory wood, soaked in water 15 minutes, then drained

Pizza

1 package pizza dough, in dairy case at supermarket

4 small leeks, white and tender green portions julienned into fine 1½-inch-long strips

2 cups sliced, smoked turkey, skin and bones discarded

1 tablespoon thyme

4 large cloves garlic, minced

4 large plum tomatoes, sliced thinly lengthwise

½ cup low-calorie Swiss cheese, shredded

Smoked Turkey: To smoke turkey breast, prepare barbecue grill according to manufacturer's directions. When coals are hot, add 3 pieces of mesquite, hickory, or other wood. Put turkey on grill rack, cover, and smoke until done. It will take at least 2 hours. Check smoker after 1 hour to see if you need more water and charcoal.

For my smoker, we fill the charcoal pan three-fourths full with charcoal briquets, light the coals, and when they begin to color, drain wood and place it on the coals.

For faster smoking, fill the water pan with hot water. Set the turkey breast on an ungreased grid, skin side up. Cover.

To check for doneness, make a small cut with a sharp knife. If the juices run clear, the turkey is done; if they run pink, the turkey needs more time.

Let turkey stand 15 minutes on a platter before slicing. Discard skin and cut meat into thin slices.

Pizza: Unroll dough. Stretch and press dough into oiled or non-stick cookie sheet.

Toss leeks with oil. Season with salt and pepper.

Arrange turkey, leeks, thyme, garlic, and tomatoes over crust. Sprinkle with cheese.

Preheat oven to 425° F.

Bake pizza on lowest rack, 10 to 15 minutes or until crust is cooked and topping hot. Cut into pieces. Serve hot.

Nutritional Data

PER SERVING		EXCHANGES	
Calories:	129	Milk:	0.0
Fat (gm):	3.8	Veg.:	1.0
Sat. fat (gm):	2.3	Fruit:	0.0
Cholesterol (mg):	17	Bread:	0.5
Sodium (mg):	180	Meat:	1.0
% Calories from fat:	26	Fat:	0.0

OLIVES AND CHEESE ON LAHVOSH CRACKERS

◆

A surprise crust is the large lahvosh cracker. Top with a few of your "favorites" and bake at 375° F. 20 to 25 minutes or until toppings are hot and cooked to taste.

◆

4 Servings

Seasoned olives
½ cup black olives, sliced
1 clove garlic, minced
2 green onions, minced
½ teaspoon each: basil, oregano, ground coriander
1 large lahvosh cracker, about 14 inch diameter
1 cup Alpine Lace fat-free cheese, grated

Mix together drained olives, garlic, onions, and seasonings in a small bowl. Cover and refrigerate overnight. Stir before using.

Preheat oven to 375° F. Sprinkle cracker with olive mixture and top with cheese. Set it on pizza rack and put on lowest rack in oven.

Bake about 20 minutes or until hot and cheese is melted. Cut pizza in half and serve hot.

◆

Nutritional Data

PER SERVING		EXCHANGES	
Calories:	184	Milk:	0.0
Fat (gm):	3.2	Veg.:	0.0
Sat. fat (gm):	.1	Fruit:	0.0
Cholesterol (mg):	15	Bread:	1.0
Sodium (mg):	178	Meat:	2.5
% Calories from fat:	15	Fat:	0.0

◆

ZUCCHINI AND WILD MUSHROOM CRACKER-PIZZA

Wild brown mushrooms tend to be costly, but they are worth it for the taste. You can use all white mushrooms or substitute larger amounts of the wild mushrooms in season. A surprise crust is the large lahvosh cracker. Top with a few of your favorites, and bake at 375° F. 20 to 25 minutes or until toppings are hot and cooked to taste. This is also good on individual whole-wheat crusts.

8 Servings

- 2 tablespoons margarine (divided)
- 2 shallots, minced
- 1 zucchini, sliced thin, horizontally
- 1½ lbs. mixed brown mushrooms, shiitake and chanterelles, thinly sliced
- ¼ teaspoon each: pepper, ground nutmeg
- 2 cups low-fat, small-curd cottage cheese
- 1 cup plain non-fat yogurt
- ¼ teaspoon mace
- 1 large lahvosh cracker

Heat half of the margarine with shallots in non-stick frying pan. Add zucchini and saute on both sides until beginning to brown. Remove zucchini and reserve.

Add remaining margarine and saute mushrooms, covered, until glazed and tender. Season with pepper and nutmeg. Set aside.

Puree cottage cheese in food processor fitted with steel blade. Mix in yogurt and mace.

Place lahvosh cracker on non-stick or foil-covered cookie sheet. Spread cheese on crust. Distribute mushroom mixture over cheese. Arrange zucchini slices in a design over mushrooms.

Preheat oven to 375° F. Bake pizza on lowest rack in oven 20 minutes or until hot.

Cut with a pizza wheel or use a pair of kitchen scissors.

Nutritional Data

PER SERVING		EXCHANGES	
Calories:	138	Milk:	0.0
Fat (gm):	3.3	Veg.:	0.5
Sat. fat (gm):	.7	Fruit:	0.0
Cholesterol (mg):	3	Bread:	1.0
Sodium (mg):	388	Meat:	1.0
% Calories from fat:	21	Fat:	0.0

Butternut Squash, Maple Syrup, and Peanut Pizza

Try this pizza for an interesting combination of tastes. Good as a vegetable side dish, with dinner, or as an appetizer. Cut into small pieces.

15 Servings
1 butternut squash, cut in half; discard fibers and seeds
2 teaspoons margarine
½ teaspoon each: sage, salt, pepper
1 package pizza dough, in dairy case at supermarket
   Canola oil, or non-stick cooking spray
¾ cup light maple syrup
⅓ cup peanuts, minced

lace teaspoon of margarine and sprinkle of sage, salt, and pepper in center of each squash half.

Preheat oven to 375° F.

Set squash in shallow baking pan, and cover loosely with aluminum foil. Bake 45 to 50 minutes or until tender.

When squash is cool enough to handle, peel and cut into ½-inch-thick round slices.

Unroll dough. Stretch and press dough into lightly oiled 15 x 10-inch, non-stick cookie sheet.

Preheat oven to 425° F.

Arrange squash circles over pizza. Drizzle maple syrup over squash and sprinkle with chopped peanuts.

Bake pizza on lowest rack of oven 10 to 15 minutes or until crust begins to color. Cut into squares and serve hot.

Nutritional Data

PER SERVING		EXCHANGES	
Calories:	115	Milk:	0.0
Fat (gm):	2.9	Veg.:	0.0
Sat. fat (gm):	.4	Fruit:	0.0
Cholesterol (mg):	0	Bread:	1.5
Sodium (mg):	227	Meat:	0.0
% Calories from fat:	22	Fat:	0.5

FOCACCIA WITH RED ONIONS AND POPPY SEEDS

*Focaccia is a pan bread made from pizza dough. It can be baked
in a cast-iron frying pan, from which it can be served directly.
This recipe reminds me of a recipe my grandmother made. It was a
wonderful flatbread with this topping. She would serve it with
yogurt spread on the hot bread.
Focaccia can be wrapped, frozen, and then reheated before serving.*

9 Servings

1 Whole-Wheat Pizza Crust (9-inch)
2 tablespoons good quality olive oil (divided)
2 cups red onions, sliced
3 cloves garlic, sliced horizontally
¼ teaspoon each: salt, pepper
3 tablespoons poppy seeds

Preheat oven to 425° F. Brush a 9-inch cast-iron skillet or baking
pan with 1½ teaspoons olive oil.

Prepare crust according to basic pizza dough recipe. With lightly
floured hands, place dough in pan and push it from the center to the edge,
using knuckles or fingers. Using your fingers or a fork, press about 10 indentations around the dough's rim.

Brush the rim of dough with ½ tablespoon olive oil.

To prepare topping, heat remaining olive oil in non-stick frying pan.
Saute onions and garlic over medium heat about 5 minutes, stirring occasionally. Season with salt and ground black pepper. Stir in poppy seeds.
Remove from heat. Cool slightly. Spread onion mixture over dough,
leaving ½ inch of plain dough around rim of pan.

Bake focaccia on lowest rack of oven 20 minutes or until it is golden
brown around the rim and cooked through. Cool slightly in pan. Serve hot
or warm.

Nutritional Data

PER SERVING		EXCHANGES	
Calories:	207	Milk:	0.0
Fat (gm):	6.3	Veg.:	1.0
Sat. fat (gm):	.8	Fruit:	0.0
Cholesterol (mg):	0	Bread:	2.0
Sodium (mg):	180	Meat:	0.0
% Calories from fat:	27	Fat:	1.0

THREE-PEPPER FOCACCIA

Focaccia is good served as an appetizer or as a side dish. This recipe doubles easily.

9 Servings

1 Basic Pizza Crust (9-inch)
3 tablespoons good quality olive oil (divided)
2 yellow bell peppers, seeded, sliced
1 green bell pepper, seeded, sliced
1 red bell pepper, seeded, sliced
½ teaspoon each: cumin seeds, garlic powder, red pepper flakes
¼ teaspoon salt

Preheat oven to 425° F. Brush a 9-inch baking pan or cast-iron skillet with 1½ teaspoons olive oil.

Prepare crust according to basic pizza dough recipe. With lightly floured hands, place dough in pan and push it from center to edge, using knuckles and fingers. Using a fork or fingers, press about 10 indentations around dough's rim.

Brush rim of dough with ½ tablespoon olive oil.

To prepare topping, heat remaining olive oil in heavy frying pan. Saute peppers over medium heat about 5 minutes.

Add cumin seeds, garlic powder, red pepper flakes, and salt. Remove from heat and cool slightly. Spread seasoned peppers over dough, leaving ¾-inch edge of plain dough around rim of pan.

Bake focaccia 20 minutes or until it is golden brown around rim and cooked through. Serve hot or warm.

Nutritional Data

PER SERVING		EXCHANGES	
Calories:	204	Milk:	0.0
Fat (gm):	6.4	Veg.:	0.5
Sat. fat (gm):	.9	Fruit:	0.0
Cholesterol (mg):	0	Bread:	2.0
Sodium (mg):	179	Meat:	0.0
% Calories from fat:	28	Fat:	1.0

SCALLOP AND ASPARAGUS PIZZA

Trim and cut off woody stems of the asparagus.

12 Servings

White Cheese Sauce
- 2 cups non-fat ricotta cheese
- ½ cup plain goat's cheese
- ¼ cup Parmesan cheese, grated

Filling
- 2 tablespoons margarine
- 8 sun-dried tomatoes, reconstituted in boiling water, drained
- 4 cloves garlic, minced
- 3 cups bay scallops, washed, patted dry
- ½ cup carrots, grated
- 1 tablespoon basil
- 12 small asparagus spears, blanched, drained

Pizza
- 1 Basic Pizza Crust (12-inch)
- 1 tablespoon dried basil

White Cheese Sauce: Mix ricotta cheese, goat's cheese, and Parmesan cheese in a bowl. Set aside.

Filling: Heat margarine in non-stick frying pan. Saute tomatoes and garlic a few minutes over medium heat. Add scallops and cook until just done. Do not overcook.

Pizza: When kneading dough, incorporate basil. Stretch and shape dough into sprayed 12-inch pizza or rectangular pan.

Distribute filling over crust and sprinkle on carrots and basil. Arrange asparagus in a design over all. Top with White Cheese Sauce.

Preheat oven to 425° F. Bake pizza on lowest rack in oven 20 minutes or until crust begins to color and topping is hot. Cut and serve hot.

Nutritional Data

PER SERVING		EXCHANGES	
Calories:	220	Milk:	0.0
Fat (gm):	5.6	Veg.:	1.0
Sat. fat (gm):	1.7	Fruit:	0.0
Cholesterol (mg):	24	Bread:	1.5
Sodium (mg):	272	Meat:	1.5
% Calories from fat:	22	Fat:	0.0

CRAB CAKE BOBOLI WITH CHILI SAUCE

♦

Honey mustard, used in these crab cakes, is one of my favorite flavorings. Add a half-teaspoon of it to a salad dressing, or brush lightly on chicken breasts before grilling.

♦

12 Servings

Crab Cakes
- ¾ lb. Dungeness crab meat, drained, flaked; discard cartilage
- 1 egg plus 1 egg white, slightly beaten
- ½ cup onions, minced
- 1 tablespoon honey mustard
- 1 tablespoon low-cholesterol mayonnaise
- ¼ teaspoon salt
- 1 cup mashed potatoes
- 2 tablespoons margarine

Chili Sauce (makes about 4 cups)
- 4 large tomatoes, peeled, seeded, quartered
- ½ cup onions, chopped
- 2 peppers, hot or mild, seeded
- ¼ teaspoon Tabasco sauce, or to taste

Pizza
- 1 large Boboli
- 1 cup Chili Sauce (recipe above)
- 3 tablespoons capers
- ½ teaspoon tarragon

Preheat oven to 350° F.
Crab Cakes: Mix all ingredients in bowl, except margarine. Shape into 3-inch flat, round cakes. Heat margarine in non-stick frying pan. Cook crab cakes, turning once, until crisp and cooked. Cool; crumble.

Chili Sauce: Combine all ingredients in blender or food processor, using steel blade.

Pour chili sauce into covered container and refrigerate until ready to use. Stir before using.

Pizza: Spread chili sauce over Boboli. Crumble crab cakes and sprinkle over sauce. Top with capers and tarragon.

Place Boboli on preheated pizza tile in lowest rack of oven. Bake 10 to 15 minutes or until hot. Serve at once.

Nutritional Data *(does not include Chili Sauce)*

PER SERVING		EXCHANGES	
Calories:	133	Milk:	0.0
Fat (gm):	2.9	Veg.:	0.0
Sat. fat (gm):	.4	Fruit:	0.0
Cholesterol (mg):	19	Bread:	1.0
Sodium (mg):	407	Meat:	0.5
% Calories from fat:	19	Fat:	0.5

APPLE AND SMOKED TROUT BAGEL-PIZZA

In the 1950s, pizza bagels first became popular. Now is a good time to take a fresh look at the idea because by slicing the bagel into four pieces, we can reduce calories. And, of course, top bagel pizzas with 1990's flavors.

8 Servings

1 cup low-fat, small-curd cottage cheese
3 tablespoons plain non-fat yogurt
⅓ cup smoked trout or whitefish, boned
4 poppy seed bagels, sliced in quarters
1 Granny Smith apple, cored, sliced into thin wedges

 uree cottage cheese with yogurt and trout in blender or food processor.

Spread bagels with cottage cheese mixture. Arrange an apple slice on each bagel slice.

Set bagels on non-stick cookie sheet. Preheat oven to 425° F.

Bake bagels 10 minutes or until hot. Serve immediately.

Nutritional Data

PER SERVING		EXCHANGES	
Calories:	126	Milk:	0.0
Fat (gm):	1.4	Veg.:	0.0
Sat. fat (gm):	.2	Fruit:	0.0
Cholesterol (mg):	10	Bread:	1.0
Sodium (mg):	306	Meat:	1.0
% Calories from fat:	10	Fat:	0.0

BREAKFAST PIZZA

Breakfast Pizza was adapted from the old ham and cheese sandwich, but this version is lighter and more delicious.

12 Servings

3 individual French breads, 8 to 9 in. long, cut in half horizontally
10 ozs. goat cheese, crumbled
⅓ cup plain non-fat yogurt
½ teaspoon honey mustard
3 slices honey ham (thin-sliced Healthy Choice), cut into ½-inch strips
4 tablespoons crushed pineapple, no sugar added, drained

Cut each bread in half horizontally.

Mix goat cheese with yogurt and mustard. Spread mixture on breads. Arrange ham slices criss-crossed over cheese, and sprinkle with pineapple down center of breads.

Preheat oven to 375° F.

Put breads on non-stick cookie sheet on lowest rack of oven. Bake 10 minutes or until hot. Cut in half and serve hot.

Nutritional Data

PER SERVING		EXCHANGES	
Calories:	334	Milk:	0.0
Fat (gm):	10.6	Veg.:	0.0
Sat. fat (gm):	5.0	Fruit:	0.0
Cholesterol (mg):	22	Bread:	3.0
Sodium (mg):	620	Meat:	1.0
% Calories from fat:	29	Fat:	1.5

ENGLISH MUFFIN PIZZA

My mother would make these muffin pizzas with cheese, tomato sauce, and oregano sprinkled on top—still a good combination. We would have these muffins for lunch on Saturdays.

8 Servings

1½ teaspoons barbecue sauce for each muffin half
    Canola oil, or non-stick cooking spray
  4 English muffins, split into halves
  2 red bell peppers, seeded, sliced
  ¼ teaspoon pepper
  ½ cup low-fat Cheddar cheese, shredded

Brush muffins with barbecue sauce.
   Spray a non-stick frying pan. Saute peppers 2 minutes. Season with pepper.
   Preheat oven to 375° F. Sprinkle muffins with bell peppers and cheese. Place on non-stick cookie sheet.
   Bake muffins on lowest rack of oven 10 minutes or until cheese is bubbly.

Nutritional Data

PER SERVING		EXCHANGES	
Calories:	112	Milk:	0.0
Fat (gm):	2.2	Veg.:	0.5
Sat. fat (gm):	.0	Fruit:	0.0
Cholesterol (mg):	5	Bread:	1.0
Sodium (mg):	267	Meat:	0.5
% Calories from fat:	18	Fat:	0.0

10.
DESSERT PIZZAS

Here, the pizza is adapted for the sweet tooth. Unfortunately, pizza has long been neglected as a dessert dish. I am extremely fond of dessert pizzas and occasionally serve them as the dessert course with a fish or meat meal.

Dessert pizzas can resemble a large French tart, and they make a beautiful presentation. Also, the delightful relationship between cheese and fruits makes dessert pizza not only delicious but a light and healthy complement to any meal.

Although I have kept the cholesterol and sugar low, the fillings in these recipes are a far cry from tomato sauce. But I have utilized tricks of the trade, such as low-calorie pudding, non-fat or low-fat yogurt, fruit, honey, and natural flavorings, to create moderate-calorie delights. Elegant, simple, and with room to accommodate your own aesthetic, dessert pizzas are a breathtaking conclusion to any meal.

MINT BROWNIE PIZZA

◆

This pizza can also be made in a 14-inch pan for 16 servings.

◆

28 Servings (2-inch squares)
1 tablespoon margarine to brush pan

Brownies
1 package (1 lbs., 4½ ozs.) light brownie mix

Topping
3 cups non-fat vanilla yogurt
½ cup fresh mint, minced
½ cup non-dairy whipped topping
½ cup fresh mint leaves for garnish

 reheat oven to 350° F. Brush 12-inch pizza pan with margarine and set aside.

Brownies: Prepare according to package directions. Some mixes require cooling brownies 2 hours before serving. Keeping this in mind, you may need to prepare brownies the day before.

Topping: Spoon vanilla yogurt into a deep bowl. Mix in mint and non-dairy topping. Spoon mint yogurt evenly over baked brownies. Garnish with mint leaves. Cut into 28, 2-inch squares, and serve chilled or at room temperature.

◆

Nutritional Data

PER SERVING		EXCHANGES	
Calories:	112	Milk:	0.0
Fat (gm):	2.2	Veg.:	0.0
Sat. fat (gm):	1.1	Fruit:	0.0
Cholesterol (mg):	9	Bread:	1.0
Sodium (mg):	92	Meat:	0.0
% Calories from fat:	18	Fat:	0.0

APPLE PIZZA

Serving hint: for a beautiful presentation, bring Apple Pizza to the table whole. This crust is special: it has a touch of raspberry and orange.

14 Servings

Orange Dessert Crust (14-inch)
    2 cups all-purpose flour
    ¼ teaspoon salt
    ⅓ cup margarine
    2 egg whites
    1 tablespoon raspberry vinegar
    3 tablespoons orange rind, grated
5 to 6 tablespoons cold water

Filling
    5 large Golden Delicious apples, or other cooking apple, peeled and thinly sliced
    ¼ cup sugar
    ¾ teaspoon ground cinnamon

Streusel
    ¾ cup all-purpose flour
    ⅓ cup sugar
    ⅓ cup margarine

Crust: To prepare crust by hand, mix flour and salt in large bowl. Cut in margarine. Dough will look like crumbled cornbread. In a small bowl, beat egg whites. Add vinegar and orange rind. Blend mixture into flour. Shape dough into a ball, cover with plastic wrap, and refrigerate 20 minutes.

Or, to prepare crust using a food processor fitted with steel blade, combine all ingredients except water. With machine running, pour water through feed tube until dough ball forms, about 10 seconds. Refrigerate dough, covered, 20 minutes.

Roll out dough on lightly floured surface. For easy handling, fold dough in half and then in quarters. Fit into a 14-inch pizza pan, coated lightly with oil or non-stick cooking spray. Prick dough with fork.

Filling: Toss apples with sugar and cinnamon in large bowl. Place apple slices on dough crust in decorative, overlapping rows.

Streusel: Use a food processor or pastry knife to mix flour, sugar, and margarine. Sprinkle streusel over apples.

Preheat oven to 425° F. Bake apple pizza 35 minutes. Crust will be light brown around edges and apples will be tender.

Cut into 1-inch slices and serve warm.

Nutritional Data

PER SERVING		EXCHANGES	
Calories:	205	Milk:	0.0
Fat (gm):	4.8	Veg.:	0.0
Sat. fat (gm):	.8	Fruit:	1.0
Cholesterol (mg):	0	Bread:	1.5
Sodium (mg):	184	Meat:	0.0
% Calories from fat:	21	Fat:	1.0

FRUIT TART PIZZA

The fruit topping of this tart can vary. This recipe uses four cups of fruit. You can substitute "fruit of the season" or fruit of your choice. For example, all four cups of fruit can be the same, or you can use raspberries, plums, kiwi, and peaches.
Serve tart soon after assembling so the crust won't have time to become soggy.

12 Servings

Lemon/Raspberry Crust

2 cups all-purpose flour
¼ teaspoon salt
⅓ cup margarine
2 egg whites
1 tablespoon raspberry vinegar
3 tablespoons lemon rind, grated
5 to 6 tablespoons cold water

Filling

1 package (2 ounces) low-calorie vanilla pudding mix
2 cups skim milk

Topping

2 cups blueberries, washed, picked over, drained on paper towels
1 cup kiwi, sliced (about 3 kiwis)
1 cup strawberries, washed, drained on paper towels, sliced

Crust: Mix flour and salt in large bowl. Cut in margarine. Dough will look like crumbled cornbread. In small bowl, beat egg whites lightly; add vinegar and lemon rind. Blend mixture into flour. Shape dough into ball. Cover with plastic wrap and refrigerate 20 minutes.

Or, to prepare crust in food processor fitted with steel blade, combine all ingredients except water. With machine running, pour water through feed tube until dough ball forms, about 10 seconds. Refrigerate dough, covered, 20 minutes.

Preheat oven to 375° F.

Roll out dough on lightly floured surface. Fold dough in half and then in quarters for easy handling. Fit into 12-inch pizza pan coated lightly with oil or non-stick cooking spray. Prick dough with fork. Bake crust 10 minutes.

Filling: Whisk pudding together with milk in saucepan. Simmer according to package directions. Cool pudding in refrigerator until set. Mound pudding on baked crust.

Topping: Arrange fruit decoratively over pudding and serve soon.

Nutritional Data

PER SERVING		EXCHANGES	
Calories:	181	Milk:	0.0
Fat (gm):	5.6	Veg.:	0.0
Sat. fat (gm):	1.1	Fruit:	0.0
Cholesterol (mg):	1	Bread:	1.0
Sodium (mg):	232	Meat:	0.0
% Calories from fat:	28	Fat:	0.0

PEACH PIZZA TARTIN

◆

The Tart Tartin was created by two French sisters at their inn. Originally, this dessert was prepared with apples and one pastry crust, inverted at serving time, with the warm apples softening the crust. Here the recipe is adapted for the pizza pan, with pizza crust and peaches. This dessert is good in the late summer when peaches are plentiful.

◆

12 Servings

Lemon Raspberry Crust

       2 cups all-purpose flour
       ¼ teaspoon salt
       ¼ cup margarine
       2 egg whites
       1 tablespoon raspberry vinegar
       3 tablespoons lemon rind, grated
  5 to 6 tablespoons cold water

Filling

       2 lbs. peaches
       2 tablespoons margarine
       ¼ cup light brown sugar
       3 tablespoons golden raisins

Lemon Raspberry Crust: Mix flour and salt in large bowl. Cut in margarine. Dough will look like crumbled cornbread. In small bowl, beat egg whites lightly; add vinegar and lemon rind. Blend mixture into flour. Shape dough into ball. Cover with plastic wrap and refrigerate 20 minutes.

Or to prepare crust in food processor fitted with steel blade, combine all ingredients except water. With machine running, pour water through feed tube until dough ball forms, about 10 seconds. Refrigerate dough, covered, 20 minutes.

Roll out dough into 14-inch circle on lightly floured pastry cloth. Set aside.

Preheat oven to 375° F.

Filling: Blanch peaches in boiling water until skin is loose, about 3 minutes. Remove peaches with slotted spoon and put under cold water. When cool enough to handle, rub skins off. Cut peaches in half, discarding skins and stones. Slice.

Melt margarine in frying pan. Mix in brown sugar, peaches, and raisins. Cook over medium heat, stirring to coat peaches, 2 minutes.

Spoon peaches evenly on pizza pan.

For easy handling, fold crust loosely in quarters. Unfold crust over peaches, leaving sides of pan unsealed.

Set pizza on lowest rack in oven and bake 15 minutes. Crust will be cooked when firm to the touch but not necessarily colored.

Remove pizza from oven. Using pot holders, carefully turn pan over onto large serving plate. Peaches will be on top of crust.

Serve warm with non-dairy whipped topping, if desired.

Nutritional Data

PER SERVING		EXCHANGES	
Calories:	186	Milk:	0.0
Fat (gm):	6.3	Veg.:	0.0
Sat. fat (gm):	1.2	Fruit:	1.0
Cholesterol (mg):	0	Bread:	1.0
Sodium (mg):	127	Meat:	0.0
% Calories from fat:	30	Fat:	1.0

CHEESECAKE PIZZA

This light, delicate cheesecake pizza is laced with cinnamon and rum.

---

20 Servings

(2-inch pieces)

Graham Cracker Crust (12-inch)
- 1 cup graham cracker crumbs
- 1 teaspoon ground cinnamon

Filling
- 3 cups non-fat ricotta cheese
- 1 cup golden raisins
- 3 tablespoons dark rum
- 1 tablespoon each: grated lemon rind, freshly squeezed lemon juice, honey
- ½ teaspoon ground cinnamon
- 1 egg plus 2 egg whites, beaten
- ¾ cup fine breadcrumbs
- ½ cup pine nuts

Graham Cracker Crust: Mix crumbs and cinnamon together. Pat crumbs into a 12-inch pizza pan. Preheat oven to 375° F.

Filling: Spoon cheese into deep bowl. Soak raisins in rum for 10 minutes. Mix in raisins, lemon rind, lemon juice, honey, and cinnamon. Blend in beaten eggs and breadcrumbs. Spoon filling over crust. Sprinkle with nuts.

Bake pizza 30 minutes. Crust will be golden and cheese cooked. Cool and serve.

Cut into 20, 2-inch pieces.

Nutritional Data

PER SERVING		EXCHANGES	
Calories:	97	Milk:	0.0
Fat (gm):	3.2	Veg.:	0.0
Sat. fat (gm):	.2	Fruit:	0.5
Cholesterol (mg):	14	Bread:	0.5
Sodium (mg):	69	Meat:	0.5
% Calories from fat:	28	Fat:	0.0

DELTA PIZZA PIE

Upon leaving Mexico, the Conquistadors took a sample of chocolate with them and introduced it to Europe. This delightful dessert complements any meal.

20 Servings

(2-inch squares)

Chocolate Crust (12-inch)
- 1 cup chocolate cookie crumbs
- ½ teaspoon ground cinnamon
- ¼ teaspoon ground nutmeg

Topping
- 1 package (2 ounces) low-calorie chocolate pudding mix
- 3 cups skim milk
- 4 ozs. light cream cheese, room temperature
- 2 cups non-fat ricotta cheese
- 2 cups non-dairy whipped topping
- 2 tablespoons cocoa powder

Chocolate Crust: Combine cookie crumbs, cinnamon, and nutmeg. Pat into a 12-inch pizza pan.

Topping: Prepare chocolate pudding according to package directions, using skim milk. Cool until set. Spoon pudding over crust.

Mix cream cheese and ricotta cheese in large bowl of electric mixer. Blend in non-dairy whipped topping.

Spoon cheese mixture over pudding. Sprinkle cocoa over filling. Chill until serving time.

Cut into 20, 2-inch squares.

Nutritional Data

PER SERVING		EXCHANGES	
Calories:	90	Milk:	0.0
Fat (gm):	3.8	Veg.:	0.0
Sat. fat (gm):	1.3	Fruit:	0.0
Cholesterol (mg):	5	Bread:	0.5
Sodium (mg):	154	Meat:	0.0
% Calories from fat:	37	Fat:	1.0

STRAWBERRY YOGURT NO-BAKE PIZZA

A lovely end to a meal. Made with fresh strawberries, this is a perfect dessert for brunch.

---

12 Servings

Graham Cracker Crust (12-inch)
- 1½ cups graham cracker crumbs
- 2½ tablespoons margarine, melted
- 1 teaspoon ground cinnamon

Topping
- 2 cups vanilla non-fat yogurt
- 4 cups strawberries, hulled, sliced
- ¼ teaspoon ground nutmeg

Crust: Use food processor fitted with steel blade to combine all ingredients; or use a spoon to mix all ingredients in large bowl.

Pat crust into 12-inch pizza pan lightly oiled.

Topping: Mix yogurt with strawberries and nutmeg. Using a spoon, spread yogurt mixture over crust.

Refrigerate until serving time. Cut into 1-inch pieces before serving.

Nutritional Data

PER SERVING		EXCHANGES	
Calories:	100	Milk:	0.5
Fat (gm):	2.5	Veg.:	0.0
Sat. fat (gm):	.4	Fruit:	0.5
Cholesterol (mg):	0	Bread:	0.0
Sodium (mg):	100	Meat:	0.0
% Calories from fat:	21	Fat:	0.5

YOGURT PIZZA WITH ALMONDS

For a stronger nut flavor, add more almonds to taste.

12 Servings

Vanilla Crust (12-inch)
- 1 cup vanilla cookie crumbs
- 3 tablespoons margarine, melted
- ½ teaspoon ground cinnamon

Topping
- 4 cups non-fat lemon yogurt
- 3 tablespoons lemon rind, grated
- 1 cup bananas, sliced
- 1 tablespoon lemon juice, freshly squeezed
- ¼ cup toasted almonds, sliced

Vanilla Crust: Using food processor fitted with steel blade, combine crumbs, margarine, and cinnamon. To prepare crust by hand, combine all ingredients in bowl and mix well. Pat crumbs into 12-inch pizza pan.

Topping: Mix together yogurt and lemon rind. Sprinkle bananas with lemon juice and mix into yogurt. Carefully spoon yogurt mixture over crust, using back of spoon. Chill until ready to serve.

At serving time, sprinkle almonds over center of pizza. Serve cold. Garnish with non-dairy whipped topping if desired.

Nutritional Data

PER SERVING		EXCHANGES	
Calories:	132	Milk:	1.0
Fat (gm):	3.4	Veg.:	0.0
Sat. fat (gm):	.3	Fruit:	0.5
Cholesterol (mg):	2	Bread:	0.0
Sodium (mg):	106	Meat:	0.0
% Calories from fat:	23	Fat:	1.0

RUM RAISIN NO-BAKE PIZZA

For chocolate cookie crumbs, simply crumble plain chocolate cookies, using a food processor, or place cookies between two sheets of wax paper and use a rolling pin to crumble them. Graham crackers may be substituted.

12 Servings

Chocolate Crust (12-inch)
- 1 cup chocolate cookie crumbs
- 3 tablespoons margarine, melted
- ½ teaspoon ground cinnamon

Topping
- ¾ cup golden raisins
- 2 tablespoons dark rum
- 2 cups non-fat vanilla yogurt
- 2 cups low-fat, small-curd cottage cheese
- 2 tablespoons sugar
- 1 teaspoon vanilla extract
- 1 tablespoon strong coffee

Chocolate Crust: Use a food processor fitted with steel blade to combine crumbs, margarine, and cinnamon. Pat crumb mixture into 12-inch pizza pan.

Topping: Sprinkle raisins with rum. Let stand 10 minutes.

In large bowl, combine yogurt and cottage cheese. Mix in drained raisins and remaining ingredients.

Spoon topping evenly over crust just before serving.

Cut into 12, 1-inch slices and serve.

Nutritional Data

PER SERVING		EXCHANGES	
Calories:	146	Milk:	0.5
Fat (gm):	3.3	Veg.:	0.0
Sat. fat (gm):	1.0	Fruit:	0.5
Cholesterol (mg):	2	Bread:	0.5
Sodium (mg):	240	Meat:	0.5
% Calories from fat:	20	Fat:	0.5

ENGLISH MUFFIN PIZZA WITH PECANS AND HONEY

This dessert is fast and easy. Be sure to serve it hot.

4 Servings

Crust
  2 English muffins with raisins, split in half

Topping
  2 tablespoons margarine
  4 tablespoons toasted pecans
  1 teaspoon ground cinnamon
  4 teaspoons honey
  1 can (10¾ ounces) mandarin oranges, drained

Crust: Arrange muffin halves on non-stick cookie sheet. Preheat oven to 375° F.

Topping: Melt margarine in small frying pan over medium heat.

Add pecans and mix in remaining ingredients. Drizzle topping over muffins.

Bake 10 minutes. Serve one half muffin per person.

Nutritional Data

PER SERVING		EXCHANGES	
Calories:	184	Milk:	0.0
Fat (gm):	8.0	Veg.:	0.0
Sat. fat (gm):	.9	Fruit:	1.0
Cholesterol (mg):	0	Bread:	1.0
Sodium (mg):	248	Meat:	0.0
% Calories from fat:	38	Fat:	1.0

11.

PARTY PIZZAS

DO-IT-YOURSELF CALIFORNIA PIZZA

California pizza is usually small or individual pizza, with thin crust and innovative toppings. Some of the pizzas have no sauce at all.

12 Guests

In a basket or on a countertop, decoratively arrange both homemade crusts that are ready to roll and prepared crusts.

157

Prepared crusts:
- 1 package whole-wheat pita bread, opened
- 1 package large lahvosh crackers
- 6 individual Boboli breads

Homemade Crusts:
- 1 Basic or Whole-Wheat Pizza dough, mixed with 2 tablespoons sesame seeds: divide into 6 balls, ready to roll
- 1 White Cornmeal Pizza dough, divided into 6 balls, ready to roll

Have available:
- pastry cloth
- rolling pin
- flour
- pizza paddle
- small bowl of cornstarch

Set out:
Double recipes of selected pizza sauces (see Chapter 5) or selection of purchased sauces, including pesto sauce.

Set out:
3 or 4 bowls of any of the following vegetables:
- yellow or green bell pepper strips
- cooked asparagus spears, green or white
- sliced tomatoes or sun-dried tomatoes, reconstituted
- chopped hot peppers
- artichoke hearts
- chopped red onions
- sauted white or brown mushrooms

Set out:
2 or 3 bowls of any of the following meats and cheeses:
- turkey sausage, sliced, sauted
- cooked shrimp
- grated Asiago or Parmesan cheese
- grated low-fat mozzarella cheese
- crumbled goat's cheese

P reheat oven with grill stone to 425° F.

Have guests assemble their own pizza. Cook pizzas until homemade crusts are light golden brown and toppings are hot. Cooking cracker and pita bread will take less time.

SUN-DRIED TOMATO, GOAT'S CHEESE, AND GARLIC PIZZA

*Sun-dried tomatoes can be reconstituted in boiling water for
10 minutes. Drain, chop, and use them in this recipe. This method
of reconstituting sun-dried tomatoes eliminates the use of
oil. The combination of sun-dried tomatoes, goat's cheese, and
garlic slivers is synonymous with California pizza. Now it's
a classic combination.*

15 Servings
 1 package pizza dough, in dairy case at supermarket
 ¼ cup fresh rosemary, crumbled
 8 cloves garlic, peeled, left whole
 ½ cup low-fat mozzarella cheese, grated
 1 cup plain goat's cheese, crumbled (or to taste)
 10 sun-dried tomatoes, reconstituted, drained
 ¼ cup cilantro, minced

 nroll dough. Stretch and press dough into lightly oiled or non-stick
cookie sheet, 15 x 10 inches.

Sprinkle crust with rosemary. Set aside.

Bake garlic, covered, at 325° F. about 20 minutes. Garlic will color
slightly. Turn once. Cool and cut horizontally into thin strips.

Meanwhile, sprinkle cheese, tomatoes, and cilantro over pizza crust.
Top with garlic slivers.

Preheat oven to 425° F. Bake pizza on lowest rack in oven 20 minutes
or until crust begins to color and topping is hot. Cut and serve.

Nutritional Data

PER SERVING		EXCHANGES	
Calories:	98	Milk:	0.0
Fat (gm):	3.1	Veg.:	0.0
Sat. fat (gm):	1.4	Fruit:	0.0
Cholesterol (mg):	8	Bread:	1.0
Sodium (mg):	79	Meat:	0.5
% Calories from fat:	28	Fat:	0.0

Vanilla Pizza with Poached Pears

You can top pizza with cut, sliced fruit if you wish to omit the poached pears.

15 Servings

Poached Pears
- 2 cups red wine
- 2 cups water
- 1 packet (.35 ounce) sugar substitute
- ¼ cup sugar
- 1 teaspoon vanilla
- 5 large pears, cored, peeled

Graham Cracker Crust
- 1½ cups graham cracker crumbs
- 2½ tablespoons margarine, melted
- 1 teaspoon ground cinnamon

Filling
- 1 package (2 ounces) low-calorie vanilla pudding
- 3 cups skim milk

Poached Pears: Heat wine with water over medium heat. Mix in sugar substitute, sugar, and vanilla. Bring water to boil. Reduce heat to simmer. Add pears and continue to simmer about 25 minutes or until pears are tender but not mushy. Drain and cool. Slice pears horizontally.

Crust: Use food processor fitted with steel blade to combine all ingredients; or use a spoon to mix all ingredients in large bowl.

Pat crust into 12-inch pizza pan lightly oiled.

Filling: Cook pudding according to package directions, adding the skimmed milk. Cool until just set. Spoon pudding over crust using back of spoon.

Fan pears creatively over pudding.

Chill until serving time.

Nutritional Data

PER SERVING		EXCHANGES	
Calories:	143	Milk:	0.0
Fat (gm):	2.1	Veg.:	0.0
Sat. fat (gm):	.3	Fruit:	1.5
Cholesterol (mg):	1	Bread:	0.5
Sodium (mg):	172	Meat:	0.0
% Calories from fat:	13	Fat:	0.5

12.

<u>GRILLED PIZZA PARTY</u>

menu

◆

VEGETABLE GAZPACHO

◆

GRILLED VENISON SAUSAGE & PEPPERS PIZZA

◆

CURRIED CHICKPEAS

◆

FRESH-CUT FRUIT

◆

VEGETABLE GAZPACHO

Still the all-time Spanish favorite cold vegetable soup. In southern Spain, the soup color is almost pink. For this effect, blend in 1 slice of crustless bread.

5 Servings
2 cloves garlic
⅓ cup onions, chopped
3 cups tomatoes, peeled, seeded
1 red or green bell pepper, seeded, chopped
1 cucumber, peeled, sliced
½ cup celery, chopped
¼ cup parsley or cilantro, chopped
2 cups tomato juice
¼ cup red wine vinegar
½ teaspoon Worcestershire sauce
¼ teaspoon pepper

U sing blender or food processor fitted with steel blade, puree garlic, onions, and tomatoes. Add remaining ingredients and process until pureed. Taste to adjust seasonings.

Pour soup into covered container and chill before serving. Soup can be garnished with chopped vegetables such as cucumbers, green onions, and chopped peppers.

Nutritional Data

PER SERVING		EXCHANGES	
Calories:	33	Milk:	0.0
Fat (gm):	.4	Veg.:	1.5
Sat. fat (gm):	.0	Fruit:	0.0
Cholesterol (mg):	0	Bread:	0.0
Sodium (mg):	233	Meat:	0.0
% Calories from fat:	10	Fat:	0.0

VENISON SAUSAGE AND PEPPERS PIZZA WITH BARBECUE SAUCE

Venison sausage is available by mail order from Wild Game, Incorporated, in Chicago. This pizza recipe combines the rich flavors of the American Southwest with the convenience of your patio.

24 Servings

Topping

    Canola oil, or non-stick cooking spray

2 cups venison, or turkey sausage, cut in thin slices

12 small Anaheim or any sweet peppers, seeded, left whole

3 red or yellow bell peppers, seeded, cut in strips

1 medium red onion, cut into ¼-inch slices

2 tomatoes, sliced

6 large cloves garlic, sliced horizontally

2 tablespoons canola oil

½ teaspoon each: ground cumin, garlic powder

1 cup low-calorie Monterey Jack cheese, grated

Pizza

2 Basic Pizza Crusts (12-inch)

3 tablespoons cumin seeds

Barbecue Sauce

1 Barbecue Sauce recipe (see page 28)

    Prepare sauce day before the party.

Topping: Prepare grill. When coals are hot, set oiled grill rack on grid. Cook venison sausage, peppers, onion slices, tomatoes, and garlic.

Mix oil with cumin and garlic powder. Continue to grill vegetables and sausage about 3 to 4 minutes, brushing on oil mixture as you grill. Turn once.

Remove food to a dish.

Pizza: About 1 hour before guests arrive, shape and stretch dough. Leave free-form or place on oiled pizza or rectangular pans. Sprinkle with cumin seeds.

Preheat pizza tile.

Barbecue Sauce: Brush each pizza crust with ⅓ cup Barbecue Sauce.

Place grilled vegetables and sliced sausage rounds on pizza crusts; sprinkle with cheese.

Sprinkle pizza paddle lightly with cornmeal. With a quick movement, place pizzas on grill.

Cover and cook 5 to 10 minutes or until crusts are light golden brown and toppings hot.

Nutritional Data

PER SERVING		EXCHANGES	
Calories:	121	Milk:	0.0
Fat (gm):	3.4	Veg.:	0.0
Sat. fat (gm):	.2	Fruit:	0.0
Cholesterol (mg):	3	Bread:	1.0
Sodium (mg):	97	Meat:	1.0
% Calories from fat:	25	Fat:	0.0

CURRIED CHICKPEAS

◆

Always buy the best curry powder available. You can substitute catsup for tomato paste.

10 Servings

1 tablespoon canola oil
1 cup green onions, minced
3 cloves garlic, minced
3 cans (15 ounces each) chickpeas, drained
2 cups tomatoes, chopped
1 teaspoon each: freshly grated ginger, curry powder
½ teaspoon turmeric
3 tablespoons tomato paste

Heat oil in saucepan over medium heat. Saute onions and garlic 5 minutes or until tender.

Add chickpeas to saucepan. Mix in tomatoes, spices, and tomato paste. Continue cooking until hot.

Serve hot or cold.

◆

Nutritional Data

PER SERVING		EXCHANGES	
Calories:	153	Milk:	0.0
Fat (gm):	3.9	Veg.:	1.0
Sat. fat (gm):	.4	Fruit:	0.0
Cholesterol (mg):	0	Bread.	1.5
Sodium (mg):	551	Meat:	0.0
% Calories from fat:	22	Fat:	0.5

FRESH-CUT FRUIT

Your favorite fresh fruits will do nicely, but try to use fruit in season as it is usually tastier and less expensive. The following represents a typical selection.

2 honeydew melons, cut in bite-size pieces
8 kiwis, peeled, sliced
4 cups blueberries, washed

 rrange fruit on plate and chill until serving time.

13.
PIZZA CONTEST

T o host a pizza competition, first ask two or three of your guests to
be judges. Have a sheet printed, with names of the contestants
and the contest categories.

The prepared pizza crusts should be on a platter or in a basket. These
could include pita bread, Boboli, or English muffins, or other small prepared crusts. The homemade crusts will be in dough balls, allowing contestants to "roll their own."

Topping and sauces should be arranged on the table and contestants
instructed to create their own California Pizzas.

The judges don't eat them, but judge them in several categories:

    A. Design

    B. Best shaped

    C. Most creative

Guidelines

1. No entrant can be a judge.

2. It is fun if there is an audience made up of some non-participating guests.

3. Take pictures of the winners.

4. Set a time limit.

5. The prize to the winner can be pizza sauce, spirited gifts, or anything you want (including, of course, this book).

6. Have a table ready to display pizzas.

7. Contestants can prepare more than one entry.

After the winners are announced, everyone is encouraged to create their own California Pizzas.

INDEX

Recipes are indexed by "key" word, omitting the word "pizza."

Eat Well & Stay Healthy
with Good Health Books from Surrey

The Free and Equal® Cookbook
by Carole Kruppa
From appetizers to desserts, these 150-plus, *sugar-free* recipes will make your mouth water and your family ask for more! Includes soups, salads, entrees, desserts, snacks—even breakfast treats. Now you can make great dishes like cioppino, Caesar salad, shrimp Louisiana, stuffed peppers, and chicken cacciatore, yet keep control of calories, cholesterol, fat, and sodium. Calorie counts and diabetic exchanges.

The Free and Equal® Dessert Cookbook
by Carole Kruppa
Make cheese cake, black bottom pie, chocolate bon bons, cookies, cakes, and much more *all sugar-free.* More than 160 delicious recipes that help you control calories, cholesterol, and fat. Calorie counts and diabetic exchanges.

The Microwave Diabetes Cookbook
by Betty Marks
More than 130 delicious, time-saving, *low fat, sugar-free* recipes for everyone concerned with heart-health, and especially those with diabetes. Easy-to-follow directions for everything from appetizers to desserts, vichyssoise to pizza. Complete nutritional data, calorie counts, and diabetic exchanges.

Thinner Dinners in Half the Time
by Carole Kruppa
Make your own diet dishes—such as Mediterranean artichoke dip, roast pork chops Calypso, chicken Veronique, and marinated salmon with pasta—then *freeze ahead* to keep your fridge filled with fast fixings. You'll enjoy better taste—and better nutrition—than expensive commercial frozen foods that are usually high in fat and sodium. Over 160 delicious time-savers. Complete nutritional data, including calories per serving and diabetic exchanges.

The Restaurant Companion: A Guide to Healthier Eating Out
by Hope S. Warshaw, M.M.Sc., R.D.
All the practical information you need to order low-fat, high-nutrition meals in 15 popular cuisines! At Chinese, Italian, or Mexican restaurants (plus many others), fast-food chains, salad bars—even on airlines—you'll *learn how to stay in control* of calories, fat, sodium, and cholesterol when eating out.

The Love Your Heart Low Cholesterol Cookbook, Revised Second Edition
by Carole Kruppa
Give your taste buds a treat and your heart a break with 250 low-cholesterol recipes for everything from appetizers to desserts. Enjoy the great tastes—with *no cholesterol*—of deviled eggs, Italian bean soup, oriental chicken salad, chocolate cake, and many more easy-to-make delights. Nutritional data, diabetic exchanges, and calorie counts.

The Love Your Heart Mediterranean Low Cholesterol Cookbook
by Carole Kruppa
Hearty, exotic, traditional, delicious—all great words to describe these mouth-watering dishes from the south of France, Italy, Spain, Greece—even Morocco. Yet the 200-plus recipes—from appetizers to desserts—are *streamlined for heart health.* Keeping the tempting, sun-drenched flavors while controlling fat, cholesterol, sodium, and calories is this book's genius! Complete nutritional data and diabetic exchanges.

Feeding Your Baby From Conception to Age 2
by Louise Lambert-Lagacé
First U.S. edition. Complete information on good nutrition for babies—and mothers—before, during, and after pregnancy. Includes breast-feeding (with tips for working moms), dealing with problem eaters, recipes for baby food. *Extensive nutritional information in plain talk.*

"Skinny" Recipes for Great Meals

Skinny Beef
by Marlys Bielunski

Over 100 healthy, *low-fat recipes* for America's favorite food. The first major beef cookbook to follow American Heart Association guidelines of 30% or fewer calories from fat. The great tastes of beef in all its varieties: stir-frys, salads, barbecues, roasts, and easy-to-make 30-minute meals that combine beef with other ingredients for delicious entrees. Nutritional data for each recipe.

Skinny Pizzas
by Barbara Grunes

Our national fun food now qualifies as our *national good-health food, too!* These 100-plus tempting, easy, economical recipes trim away excess fat, cholesterol, and calories so you can serve pizza without guilt. Includes: shrimp, spinach, chicken, teriyaki, stir-fry, vegetarian Creole, scallop, Szechwan, cheesecake pizzas and dozens more. Plus 18 pizzas for the barbecue. *Follows AHA guidelines* of 30% or fewer calories from fat. Nutritional data for each recipe.

Skinny Seafood
by Barbara Grunes

The sea's bounty affords happy, healthy eating—especially when it's prepared to increase natural flavor while controlling fat, cholesterol, and calories. These 101 creative recipes range from steamed lake trout and grilled snapper to seafood pizza, finnan haddie, scallop burritos, whole Maine lobster, Cajun catfish, Cantonese fish soup, jambalaya shrimp salad—even a Wisconsin fish boil! *Follows AHA guidelines* of 30% or fewer calories from fat. Complete nutritional data.

Skinny Soups
by Ruth Glick and Nancy Baggett

More than 100 delicious, hearty yet calorie-wise soups from elegant crab and mushroom bisque, exotic Malaysian chicken scallion, and unusual Italian garden to standbys such as French onion, chicken-rice, and New England fish chowder. *Recipes keep calories from fat under 30%,* and emphasize low sodium, low cholesterol, and high-fiber ingredients. Complete nutritional data.

Skinny Spices
by Erica Levy Klein

50 nifty homemade spice blends, ranging from Ha Cha chili to Moroccan mint, to make even diet meals exciting! Spice blends require no cooking and add *zero fat, cholesterol, or calories* to food. Includes 100 recipes that use the blends.

Skinny Cakes, Cookies, and Sweets
by Sue Spitler

It *is* possible to create over 100 low-fat desserts and sweets, *none exceeding 250 calories per serving*—not even the cheesecakes! Sue Spitler proves it with carrot cake, baked Alaska, apple pie, caramel flan, oatmeal cookies, plums in port, chocolate cake, and 90 more marvelous treats slimmed down to AHA guidelines of 30% or fewer calories from fat. Easy to prepare—delicious. Nutrition data for each recipe.